W9-BCK-608

The Ohio State University Press

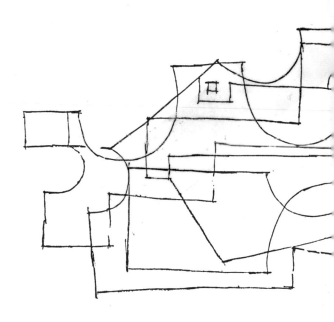

The Novels
of William Golding

Howard S. Babb

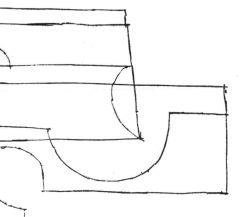

The Novels
of William Golding

FOR CORINNA AND STEPHEN

Contents

Acknowledgments

I am indebted to the University of California for an appointment to the Humanities Institute in the summer of 1966 that enabled me to write part of this book. I wish to thank Faber and Faber, Ltd., and Coward-McCann, Inc., for permission to quote from *Lord of the Flies;* I am grateful to Faber and Faber, Ltd., and to Harcourt, Brace, and World, Inc., for permission to quote from *The Inheritors, Pincher Martin* (first published in the United States as *The Two Deaths of Christopher Martin*), *Free Fall, The Spire,* and *The Pyramid.* The editors of *Essays in Criticism* and *The Minnesota Review* have kindly permitted me to use, in somewhat altered form, articles about Golding's work that I first published in those journals: a part of the chapter on *Pincher Martin* originally appeared under the title "On the Ending of *Pincher Martin*" in *Essays in Criticism,* XIV (1964); and portions of the chapters on *Lord of the Flies, The Inheritors, Pincher Martin,* and *Free Fall* originally appeared under the title "Four Passages from William Golding's Fiction" in *The Minnesota Review,* V (1965). For expert typing, I am thankful to Mrs. Betty Becker, Mrs. Mary Gazlay, Mrs. Virginia McQuaid, Miss Sue Smith, and Miss Cathy Smith. For many hours of editorial work I am indebted to Richard A. McKee.

Hazard Adams, as my chairman at Irvine, has given me specific support in a number of ways, while as scholar, critic, and person he has provided a continuing example to all of us in the department. My greatest debt, however, is to my wife and son, who have endured the writing of this book.

HOWARD S. BABB

University of California, Irvine
August, 1969

Introduction

Without much preliminary ado, I shall examine in the following chapters the series of novels that William Golding began publishing in 1954, for they seem to me extraordinary books, more so than their public reception would indicate. The first of them, *Lord of the Flies*, has proved by all odds the most successful, and Golding's fame depends on it in large part. *The Inheritors*—rather oddly, I think—has never caught the public fancy. *Pincher Martin* is much more widely known, achieving a certain notoriety, indeed, because of its ending, which reveals that the leading character has in fact died near the start of the story. But neither *Free Fall* nor *The Spire*, though published with some fanfare, has demonstrated anything like the appeal of *Lord of the Flies* for the general reader, and certainly *The Pyramid* does not seem to have captured his attention. Probably at present the body of Golding's work is more esteemed by critics than by the public. Although *Lord of the Flies* has had its detractors —in part, I suspect, precisely because of its popular success —it has generated a good deal of critical dicussion in the years since its publication, and *Pincher Martin* provoked a controversy of its own when it appeared. While *Free Fall* and *The Spire*, to say nothing of *The Pyramid*, evidently disappointed some of the critics who had eagerly awaited them, others have continued to claim for Golding a place in the first rank of contemporary novelists. And the amount of criticism devoted to his fiction continues to increase.

Despite the growing attention to Golding's work, only one book has been written which to my mind seeks to explore both the structures of his novels in some detail and their meanings in a sufficiently sustained fashion: the extremely perceptive *William Golding: A Critical Study* (New York, 1967), by Mark Kinkead-Weekes and Ian Gregor.[1] Although its authors deal intensively with each of Golding's books (up to *The Pyramid*) and provide an exemplary analysis of *The Inheritors,* they seem to me somewhat too committed in their discussions of the later stories to developing several overarching claims about differing imaginative modes—either within the given novel or in Golding's progress from novel to novel —and I also sense that they regard the conclusions to several of the books somewhat more optimistically than I do. In any case, the primary value which my own chapters can pretend to is that they attempt to make clear, through fairly strict formal analyses, the ways in which the novels develop as stories and dramatize their meanings. In this enterprise, I have taken encouragement from the words of Frank Kermode, perhaps Golding's most influential champion: "If critics have any reason for existence, this is it: to give assurances of value, and to provide, somehow—perhaps anyhow—the means by which readers may be put in possession of the valuable book." [2] In the very act of attending to the stories as closely as I shall, I am giving all the assurance I can of their value, and I trust that my discussions will enable any reader to grasp Golding's books more securely. For his novels constitute a major achievement in contemporary English literature and deserve to be better known than they yet are. He is a master of narrative, for one thing, most of his stories developing a tremendous thrust as they advance irreversibly towards an explosive climax, and one of my concerns will be to illuminate his skill in managing this typical narrative line. He is also a gifted and versatile writer of prose, capable of rendering in some of his novels an exceptionally substantial and meticulously observed physical world, and of recreating in others the inner lives of characters who range from an almost mindless Neanderthal man, through the Dean of a church in medieval England, to a twentieth-century artist. In fact, one mark of Golding's originality is his willingness to risk rather different verbal modes in several of his works; thus, in the chapters that follow I shall be insisting periodically on his accomplishments as a stylist. Most strikingly, he is a fiercely intelligent novelist who brings all his intellectual power to bear in imagining his stories, which has meant that the later ones, especially, have become increasingly difficult to comprehend on a first reading—even *The Pyramid,* so much more relaxed in manner than the earlier novels, reveals its theme only gradually and obliquely. This helps to explain, of course, the diminishing appeal of his books to the general public, and it is my excuse for dwelling, in treating the later novels, on their meanings as they unfold. Most fundamentally, however, he is intensely honest as a novelist: although a religious view of man has manifested itself more and more clearly in his fiction up through *The Spire,* for example, Golding refuses to represent his characters as transcending the limitations of the human condition. While I shall from time to time be pointing out what seem to me weaknesses in these stories, the virtues I have just claimed for Golding as novelist will indicate the perspectives from which I examine the separate novels through the following pages—in hopes of demonstrating that these virtues are indeed substantial.

1. This treatment of Golding's fiction up through *The Spire* was published shortly after I had completed my own chapters on the first five novels, and I have been delighted to find its authors confirming, for one thing, my sense of the richness as fictions of Golding's stories or seizing on many of the same ambiguities that I regard as problematic, especially in the later novels—though I think that Mark Kinkead-Weekes and Ian Gregor tend to view the ambiguities at the close of *The Inheritors* or of *Free Fall,* to name major instances, as more fully resolved than I can. But I have taken advantage of their insight to

correct several misreadings I had made of details in the novels, and no one interested in Golding's fiction can afford not to read their sensitive and stimulating critical study.

2. "The Novels of William Golding," reprinted in *William Golding's "Lord of the Flies": A Source Book,* ed. William Nelson (New York, 1963), p. 108—a collection of essays which I shall refer to hereafter as *A Source Book.*

I

Lord of the Flies

William Golding has himself supplied a starting point for discussion of *Lord of the Flies*, his first novel— published originally in 1954—and still his most popular work: "The theme is an attempt to trace the defects of society back to the defects of human nature. The moral is that the shape of a society must depend on the ethical nature of the individual and not on any political system. . . . The whole book is symbolic in nature. . . ." [1] These sentences about the book's purpose and its method do in fact indicate the main lines along which commentary on the novel has proceeded. Much of it is concerned with Golding's meaning, the commentators moving out from his statement of the theme to explore the different levels on which the story may be interpreted. Clearly Golding's words themselves here provide some warrant for reading the story variously, with their references to society, individual man, ethics, and politics. As for Golding's method, which has come in for its own share of attention, there is some difference of critical opinion, his books being called fables, allegories, symbolic structures, or even romances.[2] But the critics agree that his method, however one defines it, is radically conditioned by meaning: that the entire fictional structure—in all its details, some would say—is created with a view to its significance. Such a method, in its devotion to meaning, runs the risk of oversimplifying the texture of the virtual life that we commonly assume it is the job of fiction to render. The method would seem to pose a threat, also, to the story as a story, perhaps subjecting it to the imperatives of meaning rather than of narrative power.

Certainly the spareness of the controlling narrative in most of Golding's books and the significance generated by so many local details tempt one to talk about meaning, and I shall be talking about it throughout the chapter. But in their concern to tie down his method, Golding's critics have passed over his artistry in narrative, though acknowledging the impact of his stories. Thus I want first to bring out the narrative structures in *Lord of the Flies*. After that, I shall take up the characters in the novel, who develop according to much the same principle as the narrative itself. Finally, I shall isolate a particular scene in order to suggest how the method of the novel is realized in its language.

As our cue to reviewing *Lord of the Flies* in its main outline, we may take Golding's statement that the book deals in part with "the defects of society." For the group of boys who find themselves on an uninhabited island—as the result of a plane crash during their evacuation from England in an atomic war—try to create a society for themselves, but experience its disintegration. The society begins to come into being when Ralph blows the conch he has discovered, the children collecting on the beach. But already there is a hint of irresponsibility in the pleasure the young ones feel at the notion of "something purposeful being done"—by others (Ralph is sounding the conch, and Piggy gathering names) —a pleasure underscored by the action of one who starts sucking his thumb (p. 16). At the first assembly, the group exercises what Golding terms the "toy of voting" to elect Ralph chief, attracted to him not by any "good reason" but by his possession of the conch (p. 22). When, after the island has been explored, Ralph guides the second assembly toward determining to light a signal fire for facilitating rescue, the group bolts off after Jack—Ralph's defeated rival for the position of chief, the leader of the choirboys designated by Jack himself as this society's "hunters"—and kindles a blaze that burns up part of the island, moves the children to delight and "awe at the power" they have "set free" (p. 49), and causes the first death on the island.

Society's attempt to build shelters proves as ineffective as its effort to keep a signal fire going. Only Ralph and Simon are still on the job when Golding first shows us this world at work, the other children having drifted off to doing whatever they enjoy, with Jack devoting himself to mastering a technique for hunting pigs. The split between Jack and Ralph, discernible when they met initially, starts to emerge as a split between different organizing principles of society (among other things) when Ralph complains that Jack hunts because he likes to, "You want to hunt," while implying that he himself builds from a sense of duty (p. 61). If the pleasures of some older children reveal their irresponsibility and latent cruelty—in one scene, Roger and Maurice kick over the sandcastles of the "littluns," Roger then throwing stones to frighten a child on the shore—Golding insists that the same qualities inhere in the "littluns" themselves, one of whom keeps throwing sand at his crying playmate, while another basks in the joy of "exercising control over [the] living things" at the waterline and "ordering them" (p. 69). Appropriately enough, the first killing of a pig, which both gratifies Jack's dark pleasure in hunting and marks the initial success of the children in having "imposed their will" on "a living thing" (p. 80), costs society a chance to be rescued, for the hunters have abandoned the signal fire as a ship passes the island—and Jack smashes one lens of Piggy's glasses, the instrument of the society for lighting its signal fire, when he is rebuked for the hunters' irresponsibility.

The assembly that ensues, called by Ralph in part for the purpose of "deciding on the fear" (p. 94) which afflicts the children, dissolves into a confused dance when the children testify that they are indeed haunted. And soon their fear is embodied in the dead airman—civilization's ironic response to Ralph's wish for some stabilizing "sign" from the world of grownups—who parachutes to the island to become "the beast" in the eyes of this society. The expedition that Ralph organizes in the service of the group to discover whether the reported beast really exists, an expedition led at many moments by Jack, is itself sidetracked for a time into a hunt and dance, Ralph participating in both. Once the presence of the beast is validated—once society has thus enthroned its evil —Jack openly challenges Ralph for the position of chief in an assembly which Jack himself has called, departing to found a society of hunters himself when the group fails to support him formally.

Behaving with typical inconsequence, the children nevertheless desert one after another to Jack, whose society shows itself committed to fun and feasting, to power and its ceremonies, to hunting pigs and sacrificing to the beast—to the pleasures and terrors of savagery. The first assembly of this new group translates itself into the ritual dance eventuating in the murder of Simon, a dance in which even Ralph, Piggy, and the few still loyal to the former society take part. The split between the two societies brings on war, Jack's particular raid to bear off the last lens of Piggy's glasses leaving the remnants of the rational society fighting savagely with each other in the darkness. When these four children present themselves to Jack's group the next day, intent on holding an assembly and securing the return of the spectacles, Ralph quickly gets embroiled in a fight with Jack—who cannot stand to be named a "thief," thus to have his society publicly accused of formalizing evil. So it is Piggy who must juxtapose finally the values of the two societies that the island has known: "Which is better—to have rules and agree, or to hunt and kill"; "Which is better, law and rescue, or hunting and breaking things up" (p. 216). He is answered by the rock that smashes him to death. Jack's group, which at last includes everyone except Ralph, sets its sights on killing the lone outsider and offering his head as a sacrifice, while Ralph himself is transformed into a beast in his efforts to avoid the pursuit and the fire, which, lighted to drive him from his hiding place, threatens to engulf the island. Although Ralph and the others are shocked into regaining some sense of themselves as children by the sudden appearance, at the novel's close, of a naval officer from a cruiser that has sighted the smoke of the conflagration, Golding forbids us to imagine that civilized values have indeed been effectively restored, for the adult world is thoroughly engaged in its own war.

One rather minor indication of Golding's narrative skill is the number of ways in which his primarily expository first chapter yet anticipates the story to come. On our introduction to Ralph and Piggy, for instance, it is Ralph who strips off his clothes almost immediately, reverting more readily than does Piggy to the natural state that ultimately characterizes all the survivors on the island. Piggy is the more conscious of the adult world and of those who might have died in the plane crash—the past from which the two step forth—whereas Ralph is absorbed in daydreaming about the pleasures now lying before him of life without adults (in ironic contrast to his daydreams, as the island's society later breaks down, about the adult world that he has left behind). Similarly, Piggy announces the necessity of listing the children's names and holding a meeting, viewing the conch as a means to call all together, while Ralph simply surrenders himself to the "violent pleasure" of blowing it (p. 16). Details such as these imply what proves to be the truth: that Ralph, despite all the affection and respect that he later develops for Piggy, is at bottom much more like the other children. In this first chapter itself he is allowed to betray to the others the nickname that Piggy has begged him to keep secret; and, in a telling image, when Ralph initially learns the nickname, he "danced out into the hot air of the beach and then returned as a fighter-plane, with wings swept back, and machine-gunned Piggy" (p. 8). None of this should be taken to mean, of course, that Ralph stands already beyond the pale of civilization. When Piggy fearfully observes, in a statement that does indeed predict what happens to him and almost happens to Ralph, "We may stay here till we die," Ralph feels "the heat . . . increase till it became a threatening weight," trots off quickly to round up his clothes, and finds that "To put on a grey shirt once more was strangely pleasing" (p. 12). In a somewhat different narrative vein, the exploration of the island by Ralph, Jack, and Simon described towards the end of Chapter 1 contains the first instance of a rock being pried over a cliff by the children, an expression here of their sheer delight in exploring, though this fun also interrupts their mission. By the close of the expedition, a faintly religious air already clings to Simon through his repeated mention of candles to describe some bushes which they pass, and Jack has encountered his first pig, though he cannot yet bring himself to strike it.

In outlining the progressive degeneration of the children and noting several of the details in the first chapter that reappear in some fashion further on, I have wanted to point towards Golding's fundamental narrative method. The principle is common enough: the recurrence of some event, situation, or fact in slightly varying form, the variations so managed that the sequence generates an ever-increasing emotional intensity. The effect of an inexorable progress towards an inevitable conclusion may remind us of the gradually accumulating pressure in a novel like *Clarissa,* though Richardson works by subjecting us to a series of alternatives:

when the given set is exhausted, one possibility having come to dominate the other, the dominant possibility itself divides into new alternatives. In *Lord of the Flies,* with its strictly linear plot structure, Golding's narrative power derives not only from the carefully graded variations in any particular sequence, but from the number of these sequences that move in parallel, as it were, towards a single destination. His precise control over both gradation and parallels would seem to me indirect evidence, incidentally, of the substantial amount of fiction Golding wrote before creating *Lord of the Flies.*[4]

The variety of parallel sequences that help to structure the novel, each of them revealing some kind of regression from innocence to savagery, can be illustrated fairly briefly. Two major points of reference are the huge fires near the beginning and at the end of the narrative: the first, an attempt to promote rescue which in fact causes a death; the second, a means of promoting death which brings about a rescue of sorts. In the first part of the story, the fires that the children light are normally associated with rescue, while in the second half they are linked with cooking the killed pigs and feasting. The final conflagration, of course, not only dramatizes the literal cruelty of the children in hunting down Ralph but implies as well that the world which began as Eden has become Hell. Golding centers another sequence on the dropping of rocks: Ralph, Jack, and Simon, as we have already seen, experience a communal joy when they first send a boulder crashing down; Roger throws stones to frighten a littlun, but with an arm still "conditioned by . . . civilization" (p. 70) ; the group seeking to discover whether a beast really exists diverts itself by toppling a rock into the sea until called back to its duty by Ralph; Roger pries loose the rock that kills Piggy; finally, Jack's group drives Ralph from a thicket by heaving boulders over a cliff that smash the hiding place. Similarly, the first fight among the children is a mock affair, a testimony to the sheer joy of Ralph, Jack, and Simon in exploring: ". . . Ralph expressed the intensity of his emotion by pretending to knock Simon down; and soon they were a happy, heaving pile in the under-dusk" (p. 28). But this sequence proceeds through the arguments of varying intensity between Ralph and Jack; to Jack's first raid for fire after his own society has begun to take shape; to the twins—still members of the more civilized group—fighting each other in their sleep; to Jack's second raid, this one for Piggy's glasses rather than burning branches, which results in Ralph and the twins fighting with each other rather than with their enemies; to the fight between Ralph and Jack at the time of Piggy's death; to the total war that Jack's society makes on Ralph just prior to the novel's close. The repeated dances constitute still another motif: it is initiated by Jack's capering about when he first succeeds in fashioning a hunting mask; the motif evolves through the ritual dances that domesticate ever greater cruelty and culminate in the murder of Simon; by the end of the story, the dance has become a habitual ceremony of Jack's group.[5] Finally, the actual deaths on the island and Ralph's potential death, all so artfully spaced by Golding through the book, make up a crucially important sequence. The boy with the birthmark dies accidentally, though as a result of the island society's irresponsible indulgence in the pleasure of kindling the signal fire that gets out of hand. Simon is beaten to death by the children acting as a group, but the killing is far from deliberate, for they are caught up in a frenzied dance to ward off the terrors of a storm. The killing of Piggy is the act of an individual, one who surrenders himself to the pleasure of destroying: ". . . Roger, with a sense of delirious abandonment, leaned all his weight on the lever" (p. 216). The nature of Roger's deed is underlined by Jack's attempt, as chief, to take the act to himself—"I meant that"—and by his immediate hurling of a spear at Ralph "with full intention" (p. 217), though Roger does in fact achieve an authority rivalling Jack's through the killing of Piggy. In the final hunt for Ralph, all the children know exactly what they are doing, the whole society devoting itself to murder and human sacrifice.

The fact that all these sequences move in a single direction helps to explain, I think, the effects of clarity and simplicity that the narrative produces on a first reading. Certainly the fact contributes to the pace. The story rushes forward, with the few interruptions—such as Ralph's memories of his former life or the brief glances back to the children's first days on the island—serving less as breathing spaces for the reader than agonizing dramatic reminders of how far events have gone. But at the risk of laboring Golding's narrative method, I want to treat one last motif, the matter of the "beast," for it will show us how relentless a power can be developed through a sequence of meticulously graded variations, and the motif is also central to the novel's meaning.

The beast first appears as the "snake-thing" reported to an assembly by the boy with the birthmark, who imagines it as moving about in the dark—though this "beastie" achieves, properly enough, a kind of public definition further on when the children scream, on seeing creepers burn up in the fire that rages out of control and has killed the boy, "Snakes! Snakes! Look at the snakes!" (p. 52). On the earlier announcement of the "snake-thing," however, Ralph denies the claim flatly, while Jack, with appropriate illogic, already accommodates the irrational, saying in one breath, "There isn't a snake-thing," and in the next, "we'll look for the snake too" (p. 40). When the topic crops up again during a lull in the building of shelters, with only Simon having the courage to verbalize what Ralph and Jack do not wish to— the fear of the littluns that "the beastie or the snake-thing" is "real"—Ralph betrays uneasiness, yet remains "incredulous," whereas Jack testifies that he knows how the younger children feel and that he has experienced a sense of "being hunted" by a beast, not when "getting" the "fruit" on which the civilization still feeds, significantly, but when he is on his own, hunting to kill pigs (pp. 58–59). So far the beast has been associated with this society's fear, irrationality, and dark pleasure in wielding power—precisely the qualities that inhere, of course, in its first killing of a pig with the attendant neglect of the signal fire. It comes as no surprise that the ensuing assembly, called by Ralph in some hope of "deciding on the fear" and then settling the matter of the beast, reveals instead how pervasive the terror is. Ralph admits to his own fears, though terming them "nonsense" (p. 94); Jack declares that all the children must "put up with being frightened" even if "there is no beast" (pp. 95–96); Piggy, in keeping with his rational attitudes, denies both beast and fear, but immediately qualifies his denial—"Unless we get frightened of people" (p. 97)—in words that to some extent anticipate Simon's; Simon hazards that there may be a beast, but that "it's only us" (p. 103); when a voice proposes that Simon means "some sort of ghost" (p. 104), the children vote in overwhelming numbers that they believe in ghosts, and the assembly breaks up with Jack whooping, "If there's a beast, we'll hunt it down! We'll close in and beat and beat and beat" (p. 106). The vast majority of them having thus endorsed their irresponsibility, the children are prepared to take the dead airman who drops to the island as the beast itself.

During the children's search over the island to verify the presence of the beast, Ralph may still at bottom doubt its existence. But in the hunt that interrupts the search, he offers the opinion that the pig he has struck may be the beast, and worse, from the point of view of maintaining order, though he well knows that they should wait until daylight to conclude the search, he yields to Jack's challenge that they climb the mountain in the darkness, with the result that they cannot see the beast to be a dead man. Society's fears now translated into a substantial form, it follows naturally that Jack should break away to found a group of his own on everything that the beast represents. Indeed, the beast is enshrined as the dominant principle of Jack's society when the hunters sacrifice to it the head of a slaughtered pig. This is the head referred to by Golding as "the Lord of the Flies" (i.e., Beelzebub), the head that says, when Simon confronts it, "I'm the Beast," "I'm part of you," the reason "Why things are what they are" (pp. 171–72), and thus declares man's allegiance to cruelty, irrationality, and fear. When Simon returns from the mountain to tell the children the truth about the dead airman, they regard him as the beast, but Golding's language converts the children themselves into a beast as they kill Simon: ". . . the crowd . . . screamed, struck, bit, tore. There were no words, and no movements but the tearing of teeth and claws" (p. 183). Since society has thus taken evil to itself, the beast in which it earlier objectified its terrors—the body of the airman—may appropriately disappear from the island.

The beast becomes a permanent institution when Jack, asked by his own group whether it did not die with Simon, replies, "No! How could we—kill—it" (p. 192), his words in part refusing to acknowledge the actual killing, but also making of the beast an indestructible living presence. The raid for Piggy's glasses is so narrated by Golding that Jack's hunters are again identified as a beast (p. 199). But even more significant, by the end of the novel Ralph, the sole survivor of civilized society, has turned into a beast himself. He may scream at Jack "You're a beast" when they fight just prior to Piggy's death (p. 214). But on his subsequent flight from the hunters, he obeys "an instinct that he did not know he possessed" (p. 217), keeps wishing for "a time to think" that he can never seize on (p. 235), and at last emerges from a thicket with "screams" that "became continuous and foaming. He shot forward . . . was in the open, screaming, snarling, bloody. . . . He forgot his wounds . . . and became fear" (p. 239). In accordance with an apparently inexorable logic, the novel has rendered a civilization deteriorating step by step until it lies in ruins.

What I have said so far about the plot will have made clear the impossibility of talking about narrative structure apart from meaning in *Lord of the Flies,* and I hope to have suggested as well the varieties of meanings—social, psychological, religious—that obtain simultaneously in the story. These multiple meanings can also be traced, of course, in the main characters of the book. But before treating the characters separately, I had better state that—the opinion of many critics to the contrary—Golding seems to me for the most part successful in preventing his figures from becoming simplified allegorical types, and extraordinarily successful in sustaining the representation of the children as children. With regard to the first point, I suspect that we may be

unduly influenced by the sort of statements that Golding
makes from time to time, as omniscient author, which comment explicitly on the significance of a character: ". . .
there was a mildness" about Ralph "that proclaimed no
devil" (p. 7) ; as Jack and Ralph face each other, "There was
the brilliant world of hunting, tactics, fierce exhilaration,
skill; and there was the world of longing and baffled com-
mon-sense" (p. 81) ; "Simon became inarticulate in his effort
to express mankind's essential illness" (p. 103) ; "Samneric
protested out of the heart of civilization" (p. 214) .[6] But such
statements should not obscure the fact that, in their behavior, the children normally reveal contradictory impulses
which complicate them as individuals: Piggy, for example, is
eminently rational yet very frightened; and Ralph, though
trying to cling to civilized forms and common sense, feels the
pull of the anarchic and the pleasure of emotional release.
As for the childishness of the characters, Golding strikes me
as having taken great pains to incorporate in the run of
terrifying events a series of passages which keep insisting
precisely that the children are indeed children. One might
cite Piggy's speech when he wants to accompany Ralph on
the first expedition over the island (p. 24) , or Ralph's assertion of his leadership and rebuke to Jack by forcing Jack to
build the signal fire in a different spot (p. 83) , or the
wonderfully true-to-life scene in which Jack leaves the assembly because he is not voted chief (p. 152) . But the example I
shall quote appears near the end of the story, when Jack and
Ralph are about to fight and Piggy is about to be killed:

> With ludicrous care he embraced the rock, pressing
> himself to it above the sucking sea. The sniggering of the
> savages became a loud derisive jeer.

Jack shouted above the noise.
"You go away, Ralph. You keep to your end. This is my end and my tribe. You leave me alone." (p. 211)

Despite the encompassing terror here, the words of Jack—with their petulant emphasis on "my" and "me"—might be heard on any playground.

In terms of what the characters signify, one of the sharpest juxtapositions in *Lord of the Flies* pits Jack against Piggy, the two presented as instinctively antagonistic from the start. Although Jack turns out to be the leading force in destroying the society established originally on the island, he stands forth at first as an advocate of civilized values, inquiring for the adult in charge when he appears on the beach with his choir and later declaring to an assembly: "After all, we're not savages. We're English; and the English are best at everything. So we've got to do the right things" (p. 47). Through these opening pages too, of course, Jack betrays his delight in sheer power—by bullying the choir—and his incipient cruelty: "We'll have rules. . . . Lots of rules! Then when anyone breaks 'em—" (p. 36). Soon he realizes himself in hunting. Through this activity, Golding associates him with the abandoning of civilized restraints, "Jack hid [behind his hunting mask], liberated from shame and self-consciousness" (p. 72); with, as opposed to the rational, the primitively—even bestially—instinctive, as in "He . . . breathed in gently with flared nostrils, assessing the current of warm air for information. The forest and he were very still" (pp. 53–54), or in "there were droppings that steamed. Jack bent down to them as though he loved them" (p. 132); with the spilling of pig's blood, which Jack may at first try to clean from his hands (p. 79), but which he finally uses to initiate another hunter (p. 162). In the assembly for "deciding on the fear," Jack repudiates the organizing principle of Ralph's society—"Why should choosing make any difference?"—and utters his commitment to power, "Bollocks to the rules! We're strong—we hunt" (p. 106). This is the sort of power on which Jack's society proves later to be based, a power manifested in the ceremonial obeisance to himself that Jack requires of his tribe, and expressed in another way through those sacrifices by which the tribe creates its beast, thus sanctifying the forces of irrationality and fear that reign in the children themselves. Jack, we remember, has acknowledged his fear much earlier in the story, even though questioning the existence of a beast. And on that search for the beast which brings the boys to the mountain, Jack challenges Ralph to climb with him to the top in order to assert his own powers, his own capacity to lead—not in order to serve society, certainly not in order to outface the beast. Once the beast materializes in the body of the airman, the triumph of Jack and all he represents is virtually assured.[7]

Whereas Jack lawlessly thrusts aside the restraints of civilization, makes a principle of fear, and relentlessly pursues power, Piggy is devoted to the orderly processes of civilization, constantly brings to bear what rationality he can muster, and proves woefully weak. Even for Ralph's society he is an outsider, a comic butt because of his fatness, asthma, and dependence on spectacles—a figure already faintly discredited by his trips to the bushes when "taken short" in the opening pages of the novel. If we are to imagine him as vaguely Promethean because he provides the means by which society kindles its fires and later has "the intellectual daring to suggest moving the [signal] fire from the mountain" (p. 154), Piggy nevertheless reveals the limitations of mere rationality. He may stand out against the assembly in denying the existence of ghosts, but he thinks Simon "cracked" for intending to search out the beast (p. 158). And when confronted by the fact of his own participation—compelled by his terror—in the murder of Simon, he tries to evade his responsibility, first by explaining what has happened as "an accident" and then by clutching at the only straw left for the rationalist, "We got to forget this" (pp. 187–88). Although in this matter Piggy is less willing than Ralph to acknowledge his guilt, in the affairs of society Piggy becomes Ralph's guide, calling him back again and again to the thread of some argument about signal fires or rescue which Ralph has lost under pressure. It is appropriate that Piggy should want finally to demand his glasses from Jack on the grounds simply that "what's right's right," and that Ralph should want Piggy to carry the conch during this last stand of reason (p. 205) —as appropriate as it is that, with the death of Piggy, rationality should disappear from the island.[8]

The most striking fact about Ralph is his inch-by-inch regression—so much slower than Jack's—to savagery. To be sure, he keeps striving to preserve a civilized order, learns to value Piggy's brains and to like him as a person, is even represented as growing intellectually to some extent ("With a convulsion of the mind, Ralph discovered dirt and decay" [p. 88]), and shows himself readier than Piggy to admit his share in Simon's death. But Ralph's weakness is marked by his lapses in logic (in contrast to Piggy's physical disabilities), lapses often accompanied by the sense of emotional release that so exhilarates the irresponsible among the children. Ralph's failures in reasoning are dramatized by those recurrent sentences that trail off in "because—" (pp. 11, 89, 170) ; and, towards the end of the novel, Piggy must supply him with the logical connective itself, for Ralph can only grasp the immediate necessity:

"I said 'smoke!' We've got to have smoke."
There was silence. . . . At last Piggy spoke, kindly.
" 'Course we have. 'Cos the smoke's a signal and we
can't be rescued if we don't have smoke."
"I knew that!" shouted Ralph. . . . "Are you suggesting
—?" (p. 207)

Despite his affection for Piggy, Ralph betrays again and
again his fundamental emotional kinship with the others:
when he must force himself to look "away from the splendid,
awful sight" of the first destructive fire (p. 50) ; when he
attempts to repress his memory of the first death on the
island (p. 99) ; when, in one of the ritual dances, he is
"carried away by a sudden thick excitement" to strike at
Robert with a spear and struggles "to get a handful of that
brown, vulnerable flesh" because "The desire to squeeze and
hurt was over-mastering" (p. 136) ; or when he joins with
the other children in laughing at Piggy, who has been
burned by a chunk of roast pig, "Immediately, Ralph and
the crowd of boys were united and relieved by a storm of
laughter" (p. 178) . The knowledge by which Ralph acts at
the end of the book, when he is becoming an animal himself,
is quite explicitly instinct, the reverse of Piggy's rationality:
"He argued unconvincingly that they would let him alone.
. . . But then the fatal unreasoning knowledge came to him
again. The . . . deaths of Piggy and Simon lay over the
island like a vapor. These painted savages would go further
and further" (p. 220) . And when he comes at last upon the
pig's head on a stick, the Lord of the Flies whom Simon has
faced and gone beyond, Ralph can only hit out at the skull,
which—in a significant phrase—"bobbed like a toy and
came back," and "Then he backed away, keeping his face to
the skull that lay grinning at the sky" (p. 222) .

Simon is as much an outsider as Piggy, but for different reasons. Although he too has his weaknesses—his liability to fits and his inarticulateness in public—he constantly reveals a kindness that no other child possesses, and he is gifted with suprarational insight. A saint, Golding has called him, and Simon's charity declares itself in his comforting of Ralph, his offering of food to Piggy, or his getting fruit for the littluns. Predictably enough, he is regarded as "batty" by the rest of the children, in part because the more-than-logical truth about man which he intuits does not lend itself to sheerly logical statements; after confusingly proposing to the assembly that the beast may be "only us," he tries again with an analogy—"What's the dirtiest thing there is?"—which is morally valid, but which is turned by Jack into a dirty joke that overjoys Simon's uncomprehending listeners (p. 103). Nevertheless, Simon holds fast to his intuition: "However Simon thought of the beast, there rose before his inward sight the picture of a human at once heroic and sick" (p. 121). Alone among the boys, he insists that the beast must be faced, accepts—in the scenes with the pig's head, to one of which I shall return shortly—the fact that evil resides in the hearts of all men, and climbs the mountain to discover the truth about the beast, the truth that the others enact in killing Simon.[9]

In spite of all my references so far to the meaning of events and characters in *Lord of the Flies,* I have aimed at illuminating the power of the story as a narrative and at indicating the lifelikeness of the children. I turn at last to a single scene which evidences both these qualities, but which will show us as well how Golding's style creates a magnificently substantial world in which the symbolic values emerge almost of themselves—which will illustrate, in short, the essential method of the novel. It is the scene of Simon's first encounter with the pig's head that Jack and his group have left as an offering to the beast. The passage moves toward a climax of its own in its symbolic statement, so realistically rendered, that Simon will himself become a sacrificial victim. And the passage moves toward the first appearance of the phrase "Lord of the Flies," which identifies the Devil with society's reification of its own fears through its sacrificing to them. What is remarkable, however, is the sustained naturalism of the scene, despite its symbolic implications. The Lord of the Flies remains a literal pig's head on a stick (it does not speak aloud until the second encounter, a fact perhaps suggesting that it becomes more defined as a force, a person, to Simon only after he has recognized that he himself must be sacrificed) ; and Simon remains a child, one subject to fits and badly frightened of the object in front of him.

> Simon stayed where he was, a small brown image, concealed by the leaves. Even if he shut his eyes the sow's head still remained like an after-image. The half-shut eyes were dim with the infinite cynicism of adult life. They assured Simon that everything was a bad business.
> "I know that."
> Simon discovered that he had spoken aloud. He opened his eyes quickly and there was the head grinning amusedly in the strange daylight, ignoring the flies, the spilled guts, even ignoring the indignity of being spiked on a stick.
> He looked away, licking his dry lips.
> A gift for the beast. Might not the beast come for it? The head, he thought, appeared to agree with him. Run away, said the head silently, go back to the others. It was a

joke really—why should you bother? You were just wrong, that's all. A little headache, something you ate, perhaps. Go back, child, said the head silently.

Simon looked up, feeling the weight of his wet hair, and gazed at the sky. Up there, for once, were clouds, great bulging towers that sprouted away over the island, grey and cream and copper-colored. The clouds were sitting on the land; they squeezed, produced moment by moment this close, tormenting heat. Even the butterflies deserted the open space where the obscene thing grinned and dripped. Simon lowered his head, carefully keeping his eyes shut, then sheltered them with his hand. There were no shadows under the trees but everywhere a pearly still-ness, so that what was real seemed illusive and without definition. The pile of guts was a black blob of flies that buzzed like a saw. After a while these flies found Simon. Gorged, they alighted by his runnels of sweat and drank. They tickled under his nostrils and played leap-frog on his thighs. They were black and iridescent green and without number; and in front of Simon, the Lord of the Flies hung on his stick and grinned. At last Simon gave up and looked back; saw the white teeth and dim eyes, the blood —and his gaze was held by that ancient, inescapable rec-ognition. In Simon's right temple, a pulse began to beat on the brain. (pp. 164–65)

The visual richness of this writing and the precise diction are self-evident. But it is worth noting, first, how carefully Golding handles the scene so that we may read it as the plausible experience of a terrified boy. Thus Simon keeps striving to shut out the sight of the head, and in the next to last paragraph, for all the insight he reveals elsewhere in the story, he momentarily imagines the beast as actual in the same way that the other children do when he wonders whether it may not "come" to take its "gift." All the things that the head utters so "silently" represent, of course, the thoughts of Simon: earlier in the novel he has expressed the idea that evil is in man, though in the present context the sound of his own voice unsettles him when he declares, "I know that"; and what the head says of a "joke," a "headache," and "something you ate" are Simon's rational attempts to excuse himself from going up the mountain. Even the phrases about "the head grinning amusedly" and "ignoring the flies," though we later come to view them as something more, seem at first reading the kind of odd perception normal enough to a boy under stress. And the interior dialogue is followed immediately by our return to a physically actualized Simon, "feeling the weight of his wet hair," and to the circumstantial description of the world around him.

But we should also notice how delicately Golding roots the symbolic values in physical details, thus preparing us from the start of the passage for the explosion of symbolic meaning at its close. If the phrase "small brown image" provides a faintly religious air for Simon, the subsequent "after-image" underplays the suggestion by recalling our minds to some extent to optics. The "daylight" is "strange" primarily because of the relentless sun and the pressure Simon feels, but the setting is appropriate for the metamorphosis of the pig's head into the Devil. The fact that the head grins and ignores the flies, though a vision proper to a frightened child, is also a covert statement about the head as the "Lord of the Flies." Simon may look up for God's help, but what he looks at is simply "the sky." If the "butterflies" are to suggest souls that avoid the Devil, they have nevertheless been literal presences in the clearing before this point in the novel. The only statement that may ring slightly false in the passage (and I am not sure that it does) is "what was real seemed illusive and without definition." This must come from the omniscient narrator, for Simon's eyes are closed, and it sounds a little like a hint to the reader to be on the alert for what is morally "real," that is, for the symbolic equations that emerge clearly by the end of the passage. But even this statement, abstractly though Golding phrases it, accords well enough in its literal sense with the "strange daylight" mentioned earlier, and he actualizes the claim in the next sentence, where the "pile of guts" (the "real") is transformed into "a black blob of flies that buzzed like a saw." The climax of the scene, though fraught with symbolic significance, is brilliantly rendered in almost purely naturalistic terms. The flies move from the pig to Simon, this fact of itself identifying Simon as the next sacrifice (the tickling and playing of the flies harmonize wonderfully with the "fun" that the Lord of the Flies later preaches). Only after this identification has been made is the head referred to as "the Lord of the Flies," though the surrounding details insist that we keep viewing it as a pig's head on a stick. And when Simon finally looks at the head, what he sees are simply the details that he has seen before, though we are made to understand all this as Simon's acknowledgment that an evil principle has been enthroned in man and that he himself— such is the force of the climactic placing of "blood"—must die. The passage as a whole, then, is superbly poised between realism and symbolism, and this is the mode of the entire novel, whose statement about man is anchored in the substantial world of the island and children.

The degree to which Golding engages us in that world— partly through its substantiality, partly through the momentum of his narrative, but especially through his management of point of view—seems to me to differentiate *Lord of the Flies* radically from such a novel as Richard Hughes's *A High Wind in Jamaica*, with which Golding's story has frequently been compared. Certainly both books present unorthodox views of children (though even an admirer of Hughes may feel at moments a certain coyness in his account which is utterly alien to the tone of *Lord of the Flies*). But Hughes systematically uses his position as omniscient narrator to keep us at a distance from his fictional world, writing bits of travelogue and essays on children, presenting potentially distressing incidents in a manner—sometimes mock-heroic—that cultivates our disengagement, sustaining everywhere an adult perspective that keeps us emotionally detached. Thus his story affects us finally as an extreme version of a fable: as rather a statement about children than the rendering of a world that compels our assent to its actuality. In *Lord of the Flies*, the sorts of explicit commentary that I have now and then quoted may make us periodically aware of an omniscient narrator, yet they scarcely qualify our absorption in the events of the novel.

And it is our very absorption in the run of the story, I suspect, that explains why many readers are unsettled by the ending of *Lord of the Flies*—in which the naval officer suddenly appears on the island to take charge of the children—or indeed by the endings of Golding's next three novels. For at the close of each he does of course dislocate us by altering in one fashion or another the perspective through which we have viewed the characters during most of the books, sometimes by introducing new characters. The main objection to such endings would seem to be that the unexpected shift threatens or fractures the illusion of reality generated by the foregoing narrative, and, since that illusion is so powerful in most of Golding's writing, the shift may feel especially disconcerting. But Dr. Johnson, for one, taught us long ago in his "Preface to Shakespeare" that the reality represented in literature is an illusion, and thus that it is naïve of us to imagine a work plausible only when it confines itself to one fixed set of circumstances: concerning the unity of place, for instance, Johnson remarks, "an action must be in some place; but the different actions that complete a story may be in places very remote from each other; and where is the absurdity of allowing that space to represent first *Athens,* and then *Sicily,* which was always known to be neither *Sicily* nor *Athens,* but a modern theatre?" [10] While some readers may continue to regard Golding's conclusions as narrative misfortunes, it should at least be clear that his endings work in various ways to expand and bring home the meanings of the stories. In *Lord of the Flies,* to mention only the case at hand, the adult world adumbrated at the close is carrying on a war of its own, does not differ fundamentally from the children's world to which we have already been exposed, and so reinforces the claim about man dramatized throughout the book in the behavior of the children.

The implications of that claim are perhaps debatable, some readers interpreting the novel as determinedly pessimistic and others finding in it some rays of hope. Certainly the civilization created by Golding disintegrates in the course of the story. And if we take the children separately as representing certain qualities within any individual, the book becomes hardly less somber. For Piggy shows us that rationality alone will not sustain us; Ralph, that good intentions, a capacity for leadership, and a commitment to social order will not suffice to prevent a reversion to savagery under pressure; and Jack, that the fears, cruelty, and lust for power which inhabit every one of us can gain dominance all too easily. But Simon seeks to confront his fears and comes to accept the evil that inheres in him as well as in the other children, though he pays with his life for what he discovers. By thus struggling against and yet recognizing his limitations as a person, Simon engages in that perennial human task which is the source of man's defeats as of his triumphs— whether one regards man from the Christian perspective suggested by certain details in the novel or from a preeminently secular perspective.

1. Quoted in E. L. Epstein's "Notes" to *Lord of the Flies,* Capricorn Books (New York, 1959), pp. 250–51. The edition to which I give page references in my text was published by Coward-McCann, Inc. (New York, 1962).

2. An early essay about the novelist's method, and one of the most influential, was John Peter's "The Fables of William Golding," reprinted in *A Source Book,* pp. 21–34. Peter distinguishes between fictions, in which the writer seeks "to present a more or less faithful reflection of the complexities . . . of life as it is actually experienced," and "fables," which give "the impression that their purpose was anterior" and which, "starting from a skeletal abstract, must flesh out that abstract with the appearances of 'real life' in order to render it interesting" (p. 22). Samuel Hynes—in his pamphlet *William Golding* (New York and London, 1964) —feels that neither "myths" nor "fables" is an accurate term for Golding's novels and offers "moral models" instead (pp. 4, 6), referring at one point specifically to *Lord of the Flies* as "a symbolic form but not an allegory" (p. 14). C. B. Cox, in his essay on that novel, finds that "Golding has mastered the art of writing a twentieth century allegory," and the critic goes on to differentiate between Golding's mode and other kinds of allegory (*A Source Book,* p. 83). V. S. Pritchett uses "romance in the austere sense of the term" to describe Golding's first novels, which "take the leap from the probable [the domain of the realist] to the possible," while he insists that Golding has an "overwhelming sense of the detail of the physical world" and that "the pressure of feeling drives allegory out of the foreground of his stories" (*A Source Book,* pp. 35–36). Perhaps Margaret Walters has made the most detailed argument for regarding the novels as fables in "Two Fabulists: Golding and Camus" (*A Source*

Book, pp. 95–107) . After noting some similarities between the romance as defined by Richard Chase and the fable—"a formal clarity and coherence; a sharp patterning of experience in the light of some intuition of order; . . . situation and character . . . reduced to a kind of abstract representativeness" (p. 95) —she distinguishes between allegory, where "the cross-reference between literal narrative and a body of abstractions is usually specific, sustained at length, and rather arbitary," and a fable, which presents a "dramatic situation . . . as an *analogy* of the world at large" (p. 97) . And she lists some of the dangers which beset the writing of fables: ". . . the failure to translate abstractions into dramatic terms, which leads to explicit commentary or didacticism; the tendency to distort experience by schematizing it too rigidly; the claiming of a universal relevance that the particular situation fails to suggest" (p. 97) .

3. James Gindin's " 'Gimmick' and Metaphor in the Novels of William Golding," reprinted in *A Source Book,* pp. 132–40, is a relatively early piece on the first four novels and a seriously misleading critique of their endings. Gindin's thesis is that the conclusions are "clever tricks that shift the focus or the emphasis of the novel as a whole," that they "contradict or . . . limit the range of reference and meaning that Golding has already established metaphorically" (p. 133) . But when confronted with specific endings, Gindin keeps appearing to deny his thesis, as in writing of *Lord of the Flies,* "Certainly the whole issue, the whole statement about man, is not contradicted by the ending" (p. 134) . More important, he strikes me as mistaken in one way or another about the ending of each novel he mentions. In the case of *Lord of the Flies,* he understands the appearance of the naval officer to mean that "adult sanity really exists" (p. 134) , whereas the world of the naval officer in fact mirrors the murderous activities of the children.

4. In *William Golding: A Critical Study* (New York, 1965) , James R. Baker reports that during the ten years prior to the publication of *Lord of the Flies,* Golding completed "several novels" that were rejected (Preface, p. xv) .

5. In " 'Men of a Smaller Growth': A Psychological Analysis of William Golding's *Lord of the Flies,*" reprinted in *A Source Book,* pp. 121–32, Claire Rosenfield describes the progression of the hunters' dances in psychological terms: "Each time they reenact the same event . . . their behavior becomes . . . more cruel, less like representation than identification" (p. 126) .

6. Several critics have protested against such explicitness, viewing it as the risk built into the writing of fables and finding often that Gold-

ing's events and characters generate sufficient significance by themselves. See, for instance, John Peter, *A Source Book,* pp. 27–28 and Margaret Walters, *ibid.,* p. 100.

7. The triumph of evil forces on the island reverses the sense of R. M. Ballantyne's *The Coral Island,* a nineteenth-century book for boys which Golding has named as lying behind his own story. In Ballantyne's adventure, three English boys—Ralph, Jack, and Peterkin —survive famously on an island, upholding the values of civilization and Christianity in the face of attacks by cannibals and pirates. The relations between the two novels have been explored by Frank Kermode in "Coral Islands," reprinted in *A Source Book,* pp. 39–42, and by Carl Niemeyer in "The Coral Island Revisited," reprinted in *A Source Book,* pp. 88–94.

8. In his sustained and lucid account of *Lord of the Flies* in *William Golding,* James Baker develops a provocative comparison between the novel and Euripides' *The Bacchae.* Yet I wonder whether his reading of the play may not be slightly overinfluencing him when he writes of Golding's children: "In their innocent pride they attempt to impose a rational order or pattern upon the vital chaos of their own nature" (p. 9); ". . . . the assertion that life is ordered. . . . embodies the sin of pride and, inevitably, it evokes the great god which the rational man would like to deny" (p. 12). To my ear, these sentences ascribe to the children a degree of self-conscious effort to behave rationally and a kind of pride that one hardly feels in the story. Piggy, to mention only the most determined rationalist, seems on the whole to be hoping, with increasing desperation, that his words will be heeded rather than to be priding himself on his wisdom. But I would of course agree with Baker that the novel shows rationality to be an insufficient support for man.

9. Many critics have felt Simon implausible as a person, a figure arbitrarily determined by Golding's fable, partly because of Simon's mystic insight and partly because of the omniscient commentaries in which Golding himself articulates some of his character's intuitions (see, for instance, John Peter, *op. cit.,* pp. 27–28 or Margaret Walters, *ibid.,* p. 100). To my mind, Simon radically offends against credibility only when he prophesies that Ralph will return safely to civilization, a prediction that lacks even narrative importance so far as I can see. Other readers have found the two scenes in which Simon confronts the pig's head on a stick dramatically unconvincing. But in the first of these, as I shall try to show in my text, Golding seems to me eminently successful in keeping Simon a terrified little boy despite the scene's symbolic overtones. Only in the second, when Simon's fit is rapidly

coming on, does Golding permit the head to speak openly; so the fact of its addressing the boy may be viewed naturalistically as a symptom of Simon's illness.

Although C. B. Cox thinks Simon "perhaps the one weakness" in *Lord of the Flies* (*A Source Book,* p. 87), he movingly discusses the .passage in which the boy's dead body is drawn off to sea to suggest that Simon is transfigured in it: that Golding achieves through "the brilliantly realistic description of the advancing tide" a representation of "all the beauty of the world which promises eternal reward to those who suffer," and thus makes the reader "aware of the Christian meaning underlying the story" (p. 86). The effect which Cox indicates here, of muted symbolic values arising out of a pervasively circumstantial description, is the same sort of effect that I go on to examine in the scene where Simon first views the sow's head impaled on a stick.

10. *Criticism: The Major Texts,* ed. W. J. Bate (New York and Burlingame, 1952), pp. 214–15.

II

The Inheritors

The Inheritors, William Golding's second novel, has enjoyed nothing like the success of *Lord of the Flies.* Although it appeared in England originally in 1955, one year after Golding's first book, *The Inheritors* had to wait seven years for publication in America—until its author had gained a reputation through *Lord of the Flies,* I should guess, and perhaps a certain notoriety through debates about the ending of *Pincher Martin,* the story that followed *The Inheritors,* yet came out in America five years before the second novel.[1] This delay in its republication and the book's relative lack of success are nevertheless somewhat surprising. For *The Inheritors* has all the narrative drive of *Lord of the Flies,* and its verbal texture—though to some degree complicated by the fact that we view events for the most part over the shoulder or through the mind of a Neanderthal man named Lok—makes much lighter demands on the reader than does the texture of *Pincher Martin.* Moreover, *The Inheritors* seems to me far and away the warmest, the most immediately moving, of Golding's novels, a point I want to stress throughout the discussion that follows. No doubt Golding engages our emotions chiefly through associating us, via the story's point of view, with a group of fundamentally innocent and good-hearted Neanderthal people—more winning from the start than the children in *Lord of the Flies*—whose fate it is to be destroyed (or captured), one after another, by a tribe of new men, by Homo sapiens. But I think that Golding also accomplishes an extraordinary feat in compelling us at last to sympathize with the new men themselves, despite the cruelty they have shown, when he shifts us in his final chapter to the mind of one of them, who is reflecting on what has happened. The effect of this ending and its significance for the meaning of *The Inheritors* I shall examine towards the close of my own chapter. But first I turn once again to

Golding's narrative art: to sketch the basic structure of *The Inheritors;* to dwell on the sorts of narrative surprise and the pathos that Golding achieves here through the very limitations of his chosen point of view; and to consider briefly his final representation of Lok, that wonderful passage in the next-to-last chapter of the novel where Golding frees us for the first time from Lok's perspective and prepares the way for the ultimate shift to the perspective of the new men.

In one narrative respect, *The Inheritors* duplicates *Lord of the Flies,* for the Neanderthal people are exterminated by Homo sapiens as gradually and remorselessly as Ralph's society is destroyed by Jack's. Early in the story the new men indirectly cause the death of Mal, the chief of the people, by removing a log from the trail, with the result that Mal falls in the water; soon they kill Ha, whom they come across as he hunts wood; then they raid the people's cave, murdering Nil and the old woman as well as capturing the young girl named Liku and the baby; next they eat Liku; after that the woman called Fa dies, swept over a waterfall when the new men prevent her from recapturing the baby; finally Lok, the sole survivor of the people, is left to die alone, with nothing to live for after the murderous visitation of the new men. This inexorable narrative sequence in *The Inheritors* is matched by another—the series of rituals and sacrifices performed by the new men—which piles horror on horror. When we first see the new men for any sustained period on their island, they are bowing down to their chief, who is miming "a rutting stag" (p. 128) ; at their second ritual, intended to promote the success of the hunters in killing a stag for food, they cut off a finger from one of their tribe; when the hunt fails, they devour Liku; and they try at last to propitiate the Neanderthal people, whom they fear, by sketching a figure of the people and staking to the sketch a young girl of their own as a living human sacrifice.

But the fundamental informing structure of *The Inheritors* is the series of contrasts that Golding develops between the Neanderthal people and the new men: contrasts which in the main ally Neanderthal man with what we ordinarily think of as distinctively human qualities and virtues, ironically enough, and which ally Homo sapiens with inhuman savagery.[2] The Neanderthal people are making their annual trek to their summer home when they meet up with the new men; the latter are fleeing from the rest of their tribe because Marlan, their chief, has stolen Vivani, the wife of another. The people are everywhere full of sympathy, as is revealed, for example, by the way in which they huddle about the sick Mal in order to warm and comfort him; the behavior of the new men is shot through with animosity, the most dramatic instance being the enmity towards Marlan of Tuami, who periodically sharpens a piece of ivory with the intent of killing his chief. The people are radically unselfconscious; Vivani is shown dressing her hair and self-consciously adjusting her fur to cover her when approached by Tuami. The people are loyal to their chief, even to the point of carrying out an order of questionable wisdom; the new men are near open rebellion against their chief, who cannot always keep them under control even by the bribes he gives them of intoxicating drink and of Liku's flesh. The people eat what nature provides—fungi, grubs, honey—allowing themselves meat only when it has been killed by some other agent and its blood drained; the new men hunt to kill their food and engage in cannibalism. The people worship Oa, a creative female divinity whom they speak of as having produced the earth and themselves; they have an almost Biblical tradition, including a story about an Edenic past and a catalogue of the names of former chiefs; and the scene in which Fa makes an offering to Oa on behalf of the dying Mal is fraught with an awful grandeur. The religion of the new men, however, is associated with ceremonies honoring the fraudulent imitation of a stag, with magic, with hunting and bloody sacrifice. The people seek each other in love; the new men devour each other in lust, biting and tearing each other as they satisfy themselves or teasing themselves quite consciously in subtle sexual games. The people are at a constitutional disadvantage through being trapped within their instincts, winning as those instincts are; the new men are ingenious in their rationality, capable of fashioning murderous weapons or of achieving a portage through rolling their dugouts uphill on logs. Above all, the people are essentially friendly, ready to greet the new men and convinced that "People understand each other" (p. 72) ; in spite of all that they suffer at the hands of the new men, they remain strongly attracted to them. The new men appear essentially antagonistic—our first close-up of Homo sapiens is of a man shooting at Lok (p. 106) —and they are animated throughout the story by a desperate fear of the people.

Although I would not wish to press the point, it appears to me that this contrast between the two groups is at least faintly articulated in Golding's naming of some of his characters. "Liku" (as in "I like you") seems appropriate to the cheerful girl who, even when captured by the new men, becomes friendly with their young girl; and perhaps "Mal" betokens the illness and unluckiness of the people's chief, though the name's suggestion of evil would be out of place for this dignified leader unless loosely applied to the bad judgments that he sometimes makes. "Marlan," the name of the new men's chief, sounds like a combination of "Mal" with Merlin, and this leader proves in fact to be an evil magician. Vivani is as full of life as her name implies. "Tuami" (which combines "you" and "friend") appears to be mainly ironic, given this new man's antagonism towards the people, his lust for Vivani, and his enmity towards his own chief—and ironic on another level when he indeed becomes our friend, both our point of view and a man like ourselves, in the novel's final chapter. The names that Lok confers on some of the other new men—"Pine-tree," "Chestnut-head," "Bush"—also work to some degree ironically to dehumanize these people. But "Tanakil," I should confess, seems too ominous a name for the one of the new people who becomes friendliest with Liku, though its shading is not too ominous for the activities of the new men in general.

Even if the names lack the coloring that I sense in them, clearly the contrast itself between the two groups is so sustained as to become the dominant shaping force of Golding's novel, governing our response to its events, characters, and meaning. But I had better add immediately, before going on to explore other aspects of Golding's narrative art, that the contrast as I have spelled it out contains the fundamental truth about Neanderthal man and Homo sapiens in *The Inheritors,* but not the whole truth. For the people are not quite so innocent, nor the new men so unrelievedly vicious, as I have painted them. For the sake of plausibility, it may be, Golding ascribes faintly evil thoughts and rather unsavory practices to the people from time to time, as in the "mixture of darkness and joy" that Lok experiences at the prospect of eating meat (p. 56), or in the people's habit of eating from the head and bones of a dead chief to gain wisdom and strength (pp. 87, 89). For the sake of the novel's meaning—to mark the evil ascendancy of the new men—Golding also allows Lok and Fa to reenact the Fall of Man in one passage; but the contentiousness and lust that they exhibit after drinking the new men's liquor do not stay with them, and the passage finally affects us, I think, as differentiating a temporary lapse on the part of the people from the permanent condition of the new men. But most important is Golding's qualification of our attitude towards Homo sapiens: in the interests of ultimately thrusting his story and meaning home to the hearts of his readers—who are men themselves, after all—he must make it possible for us to ally ourselves emotionally to some degree with the new men. Thus he gradually reveals how much they have in common with the Neanderthal people, despite the dissimilarity between the groups. The new men, we come to discover, are more frightened of the people than the people are of them. The new men suffer from famine, while the people are beset by hunger. For all their superiority and knowledge, the new men appear weak, naïve, and defenseless at many moments: consider the deflating details at the end of that first ceremony which has so impressed Lok and Fa—"The stag began to turn and they saw that his tail was dead and flapped against the pale, hairless legs. He had hands" (p. 128)—or the confidence of the new men when they set up a camp to wall out the people, utterly unaware that Lok and Fa are sitting in a tree right above them (p. 143). Like the people, the new men can experience joy in working together (p. 144). Although they feel a certain aversion to the baby they have stolen from the people, they are even more strongly attracted by it. Indeed, Vivani herself has wanted the baby to make up for a child she had lost, a fact that parallels her roughly with Fa, who has in the past lost a child of her own; and when Marlan tries to take the baby for the tribe to eat, Vivani "snapped at his hand with her mouth as any woman would" (p. 168). Similarly, the mother of Tanakil—the young girl who becomes friendly with the captured Liku, though also beating her in a passage that parallels Tanakil with the other new men (p. 162) —struggles as frantically to save her daughter when the girl is offered as a sacrifice to the people as Lok and Fa struggle to save Liku and the baby from the new men. Through these details and others like them, the new men make their muted claims upon our sympathy and thus lay the groundwork for the effect of the final chapter in *The Inheritors,* an effect that we will be in a better position to appreciate after we look more closely at Golding's narrative mode in the major part of the novel.

Every reader of *The Inheritors* will remember such features as the impact of the scene in which Lok is suddenly confronted with the mutilated body of the old woman rising toward him through the water, or the excruciating suspense that Golding maintains through long segments of the story: in the gradual manifestation of the new men through ambiguous details in the first pages of the book, in the continuing threat to Lok and Fa as they occupy a tree within the new men's camp, in the running question through the last part of the novel—for the person first reading the story, anyway—of what has happened to Liku. In large measure, these effects depend upon Golding's manipulation of the story's point of view. He confines us pretty exclusively to the perspective of the Neanderthal man Lok, a being who lives in his acute senses and often generous feelings, but one who can hardly be said to think, and who is therefore almost devoid of self-consciousness. The vividness of Lok's sensuous experience is brilliantly rendered in the prose of the novel—even in the relatively omniscient commentaries, Golding usually sustains a primitivistic aura through the details that he cites and the phrases that he chooses to describe them—and Lok's intellectual limitations make possible a host of narrative surprises.

To illustrate the normal mode of the novel and the sort of surprise that it can produce, I choose a couple of paragraphs near the beginning of *The Inheritors* (pp. 24–26). The people are climbing toward their summer home, a cave next to a waterfall, with an island in the river below. The old woman is carrying in her arms a "burden," which, we learn only later, contains fire. The narrative wallop of the episode, as we come to understand more fully further on in the story, derives from the fact that Lok falls as inexplicably as he does because he has actually smelled a fire on the island, the fire of man, a creature of whom Lok is unaware and whose presence is here hinted at for the second time in the novel. But the first paragraph I quote is the omniscient author's, which helps to set the stage for Lok's fall:

> The trail gained height at each step, a dizzy way of slant and overhang, of gap and buttress where roughness to the foot was the only safety and the rock dived back under, leaving a void of air between them and the smoke [i.e., the "spray" of the falls] and the island. Here the ravens floated below them like black scraps from a fire, the weed-tails wavered with only a faint glister over them to show where the water was: and the island, reared against the fall, interrupting the sill of dropping water, was separate as the moon. The cliff leaned out as if looking for its own feet in the water. The weed-tails were very long, longer than many men, and they moved backwards and forwards beneath the climbing people as regularly as the beat of a heart or the breaking of the sea.

There is no need for me to labor the unpretentious vividness
of this description—where some details are realized visually,
others put in motion for us, and still others related to our
sensory experience of dizziness or "roughness"—although I
may add that this passage is surpassed by many parts of the
book in which Golding achieves rich synaesthetic effects. But
this description is typical of *The Inheritors* in its frequent
animation of nature (the sort of nature Lok would see) :
"the rock dived back under"; "the island, reared against the
fall"; "the cliff leaned out." And Golding's figurative language is kept appropriate to the perceptions of a primitive:
"like black scraps from a fire"; "as if looking for its own
feet"; "as regularly as the beat of a heart or the breaking of
the sea." The description also conveys, we should notice
finally, subdued hints about the cause of the accident soon to
befall Lok: in associating "smoke," though it is the smoke of
mist, with "the island," and in referring to "fire," though in
a simile.

The people reach a platform of rock overlooking the river,
and the old woman briefly rests her burden. Lok first turns
out to view the island, then turns back to Fa, eager to share
his joy with her at being so near home and promising to
"find food." This is what happens to him:

Mentioning food made his hunger as real as the smells. He
turned again outwards to where he smelt the old woman's
burden. Then there was nothing but emptiness and the
smoke of the fall coming towards him from the island. He
was down, spread-eagled on the rock, toes and hands grip-
ping the roughness like limpets. He could see the weed-
tails, not moving but frozen in an instant of extreme
perception, beneath his armpit. Liku was squawking on

the platform and Fa was flat by the edge, holding him by the wrist, while the new one struggled and whimpered in her hair. The other people were coming back. Ha was visible from the loins up, careful but swift and now leaning down to his other wrist. He felt the sweat of terror in their palms.

The first sentence is not a casual expression but literally true, reminding us that, for the primitive Lok, words are much nearer to being things than the abstractions they are for us. So Lok turns instinctively to where he smells fire—the old woman's, he supposes, but actually man's—and he falls. The very process of his fall is recorded in the sentence about "nothing but emptiness," even this void gaining circumstance through being connected with "the smoke of the fall," a smoke which is itself put in motion, which is "coming towards him." Once "down," he holds tight to mere "roughness," the undifferentiated term suggesting how little Lok has to hold on to. And his situation is dramatized through a variety of sense impressions: the sight of the "weed-tails," the sound of Liku, the motions of the other people, the feel of "sweat." Clearly the passage forces us to share Lok's perspective as he grips the side of the cliff, but it also renders for us the quality of his mind—rather, of his mindlessness. For in inhabiting Lok here, we are in a sense inhabiting a vacuum. Everything is referred by Lok to the outer world, since he remains quite unselfconscious about his experience: the "smoke" is "coming towards him"; the "weed-tails," though really in perpetual movement, are suddenly "frozen"; "Fa was . . . holding him"; "the other people were coming back"; "the sweat of terror" is not in Lok's but in "their palms."

The paragraphs just cited will have conveyed, I trust,

something of the way in which Golding re-creates the texture
of Lok's life and some sense of the narrative mystification
and shock that the author secures through limiting us to
Lok's perspective. But I am less sure that the two passages
now to be mentioned will convey, in isolation from the story,
the pathos that Golding can also command precisely through
stressing the limitations to which Lok is subject. In the first
passage, which occurs just after Nil has announced the disappearance of Ha (who has been killed by Homo sapiens), the
people cannot comprehend the fact because so many memen-
tos of Ha still surround them:

> . . . they stood still and meditated formlessly the picture
> of no Ha. But Ha was with them. They knew his every
> inch and expression, his individual scent, his wise and
> silent face. His thorn bush lay against the rock, part of the
> shaft water-smooth from his hot grip. The accustomed
> rock waited for him, there before them was the worn mark
> of his body on the earth. All these things came together in
> Lok. They made his heart swell, gave him strength as if he
> might will Ha to them out of the air.
> Suddenly Nil spoke.
> "Ha is gone." (p. 68)

Trapped by the vividness of their sensuous awareness, the
people here imagine Ha as lingering on, though the reader is
well aware of the actual death.

Even more moving is the description of Lok's behavior
shortly after he has heard the screams of the captured Liku
and seen the dead body of the old woman in the river. At
first he tries to pull himself together and behave purpose-
fully; but soon the strained "grin" of his utter despair returns, and he is overwhelmed with sadness, reenacting a

scene earlier in the novel where he swung the laughing Liku on the branch of a tree:

> Then he began to run down river, not fast, but keeping as near to the water as he could. He peered seriously into the bushes, walked, stopped. His eyes unfocused and the grin came back. He stood, his hand resting on the curved bough of a beech and looked at nothing. He examined the bough, holding it with both hands. He began to sway it, backwards and forwards, backwards and forwards, faster and faster. The great fan of branches on the end went swishing over the tops of the bushes, Lok hurled himself backwards and forwards, he was gasping and the sweat of his body was running down his legs with the water of the river. He let go, sobbing, and stood again, arms bent, head tilted, his teeth clenched as if every nerve in his body were burning. The wood pigeons went on talking and the spots of sunlight sifted over him. (p. 111)

Remarkable in these sentences is the degree to which Golding makes the action itself—the emotional outlet appropriate to a primitive being—expressive. The action becomes so expressive in part because Golding changes the pace here—a static pose gives way to frantic movement, which is in turn marked off by the final moment of arrest—and in part because he refuses to comment explicitly on the emotional values of the scene, except for the one word "sobbing" towards the close. The mere deed of Lok's shaking the tree communicates all his yearning for the happy game he has previously shared with Liku and his despair at having lost her; yet Golding underplays even this parallelism by not permitting Liku to be named, as if Lok himself were not quite conscious of what he feels.

For the final narrative effects to which I want to draw attention, Golding capitalizes on the intense sympathy of the Neanderthal people, a quality which makes them every- where more attractive than Homo sapiens but which ironi- cally proves, in the second incident to which I shall refer, a limitation as well.[3] The first episode works in a reasonably straightforward way. Lok goes out into the night in an at- tempt to discover what has happened to Ha, comes across the scent of something "other," and responds so acutely, as he follows the track, to every hint of the other's behavior that he is "turned . . . into the thing that had gone before him" (p. 77). The details of Lok's journey indicate to us some- thing of the fear and surreptitiousness of the other being, but the episode is so handled that we are as surprised as Lok when he at last finds himself peering down at the Neander- thal people in their cave, spying on them as we now realize the new man has spied. Aside from the local drama of this conclusion, Golding uses Lok's temporary identification with the new men to underline their alienation from the people and, once again, the people's sympathy for each other: "He was cut off and no longer one of the people; as though his communion with the other had changed him he was differ- ent from them and they could not see him. . . . he felt his difference and invisibility as a cold wind that blew on his skin. The other had tugged at the strings that bound him to Fa and Mal and Liku and the rest of the people. The strings were not the ornament of life but its substance. If they broke, a man would die" (p. 78) .

The second passage reveals, ironically, a lack of utter sympathy between Lok and Fa. They are in the tree, above the new men's camp, and Lok has just awakened from a sleep during which—as we later learn for sure—Fa has watched Homo sapiens devour Liku. He asks:

"What is it?"

Fa did not move. A kind of half-knowledge, terrible in its very formlessness, filtered into Lok as though he were sharing a picture with her but had no eyes inside his head and could not see it. . . . It pushed into him, displacing the comfortable feeling of after sleep, the pictures and their spinning, breaking down the small thoughts and opinions, the feeling of hunger and the urgency of thirst. He was possessed by it and did not know what it was.

.   .   .   .

"Oa did not bring them out of her belly."

At first the words [of Fa] had no picture connected with them but they sank into the feeling and reinforced it. Then Lok peered through the leaves again for the meaning of the words and he was looking straight at the fat woman's mouth. She was coming towards the tree, holding on to Tuami, and she staggered and screeched with laughter so that he could see her teeth. They were not broad and useful for eating and grinding; they were small and two were longer than the others. They were teeth that remembered wolf. (pp. 173–74)

Attuned to Fa though he is, Lok's sympathetic intuition is not great enough to permit him to grasp the deed of cannibalism that she has witnessed—put in other terms, his humanity is too great to allow him to imagine such an act. When he searches in the last paragraph for the meaning of Fa's words, what he sees are the "mouth" and "teeth" that convey to him only superficial physical differences between the new men and the people. But to the reader, this close-up of "mouth" and "teeth" conveys a portentous, though not yet unambiguous, indication of the fate of Liku, a fate that dramatizes the anything but superficial difference between Neanderthal man and Homo sapiens.

Although it is true that the characteristic narrative effects of *The Inheritors* which I have just been describing derive from the very limitations in awareness of Lok and the people, I should make it clear that Golding does in fact distinguish several different levels, as the novel advances, in what might be called the intellectual life of his Neanderthal men. They communicate either by speech—already something of an abstraction for them, "She asked a question of Ha and he answered her with his mouth" (p. 13)—or by presumably more primitive means, "Ha looked his question at the old man" (p. 17). Their mental activity consists largely of "pictures," the term implying how closely they are bound to their sensuous experience, though these "pictures" may arise from emotions as well. While the mindlessness of the people marks a limitation, it can also indicate their instinctive oneness, their total community: ". . . there was silence again and one mind or no mind in the overhang"; then, "Quite without warning, all the people shared a picture [of Mal's suffering] inside their heads" (p. 38). Fa is the most intellectually inventive of them, trying to imagine growing food for the people in one passage (p. 49) and to imagine irrigation—I owe the latter point to Mark Kinkead-Weekes and Ian Gregor, *William Golding*, p. 82—in another (p. 62). After the death of Mal, Lok laments his inability to think consecutively: "He wished he could ask Mal what it was that joined a picture to a picture so that the last of many came out of the first" (p. 96). Further on, we see both Fa and Lok gripped by associative processes that do indeed connect disparate events, though neither one of them can really seize on the interrelationship. In seeking to define her sense that the arrow which the new men shot at Lok may be a sign of hostility rather than a gift, Fa can only mumble, "We throw stones at the yellow ones," and then repeat vaguely, "The twig" (p. 119). When Lok thrusts a stick into a bone for marrow, "He had a sudden picture of Lok thrusting a stick into a crack" to find honey for Liku, who is now a captive, and "A feeling rushed into him like a wave of the sea, swallowing his contentment in the food" (p. 119). Later on, Lok does in fact achieve his first relatively abstract thought via association, but, ironically enough, it proves wrong. He has earlier observed the new men draw up their dugouts from the river, the "picture" referred to in the first sentence, and now watches them as they work with the dugouts again:

> All at once he had a picture of the hollow logs nosing up the bank and coming to rest in the clearing. . . . There were no more logs in the river, so no more would come out of it. He had another picture of the logs moving back into the river and this picture was so clearly connected in some way with the first one and the sounds from the clearing that he understood why one came out of the other. This was an upheaval in the brain and he felt proud and sad and like Mal. (p. 191)

Lok may accurately use the causal connective "so" in the second sentence, but his deduction about the dugouts being returned to the river is quite untrue, for the new men are embarking on a portage, something Lok cannot comprehend (p. 192). The highest level of thought which Lok attains is the self-conscious manipulation of analogy: ". . . in a convulsion of the understanding Lok found himself using likeness as a tool as surely as ever he had used a stone to hack at sticks or meat" (p. 194). But he can employ "likeness" only to formulate, in terms of what he has already experienced, how different the new men are from his own kind: "They are like the river and the fall, they are a people of the fall; nothing stands against them" (p. 195). Indeed they are different. And Golding, by forcing us to participate for so much of the novel in the limited awareness of Lok and the Neanderthal people, not only intensifies our emotional allegiance to them but makes us recognize how inevitable is their ultimate destruction by the rational, self-conscious new men.

No one while first reading *The Inheritors,* I suspect, imagines being compelled to feel more acutely for Lok than he has through all those pages in which he has been associated with Lok's perspective. Yet this is exactly what Golding accomplishes in the passage, at the close of the novel's next-to-last chapter, that gives us our final sight of Lok, surely the most moving pages in Golding's fiction (pp. 216–22). He charges the passage in various ways. For one thing, Lok is left utterly alone here at the end of a string of catastrophes that has deprived him, one after another, of all the Neanderthal people—and even of the new men, whose "hollow log," as Golding notes at the beginning of the passage, "was a dark spot on the water towards the place where the sun had gone down." Moreover, Golding increases our sense of Lok's isolation by taking us away from him as well: by shifting the point of view so that, for the first time in the novel, we see Lok as the new men have seen him, as a "red creature." This new perspective is sustained, not only through references to a "creature" which is now designated as "it," but through phrasings that reflect the understanding of ordinary man rather than the perceptions of a primitive: the cave where the people have lived shows "evidence of occupation"; the "logs" and "strips of thick and twisted hide" (p. 208) that Lok has watched the new men use now become "rollers" and "ropes"; a smashed trail is likened to "a cart-track." And the shift in perspective is heartbreaking, not simply because it separates us from Lok, but because in the whole passage Golding recapitulates so much that has happened in the story, adverting now in a drily factual manner to events and situations that have become saturated with emotion for us. Thus, the creature keeps looking out at a mere tree floating away in the river, but it is the tree that has carried Fa over the fall to her death. Or the creature "came to a clearing . . . beneath a dead tree," but for us it is *the* dead tree, fraught with the experiences of Lok and Fa as they watched the new men from it. Most poignantly of all, the creature searches out "a small, white bone" in the earth with its "right forepaw," a bone which finally reveals to Lok, we realize, that Liku has been eaten—and Golding proceeds straight on from the phrase about the bone to his most detailed factual description of Neanderthal man as he appears to Homo sapiens: "It was a strange creature, smallish, and bowed. . . ." Throughout these pages, then, the cultivated impersonality of Golding's account acts to intensify our response to the Lok we have known.[4] A final description of the creature weeping will show Golding's method in miniature:

> There was light now in each cavern [where the eyes, which have been closed, are hidden in the creature], lights faint as the starlight reflected in the crystals of a granite cliff. The lights increased, acquired definition, brightened, lay each sparkling at the lower edge of a cavern. Suddenly, noiselessly, the lights became thin crescents, went out, and streaks glistened on each cheek. The lights appeared

again, caught among the silvered curls of the beard. They hung, elongated, dropped from curl to curl and gathered at the lowest tip. The streaks on the cheeks pulsed as the drops swam down them, a great drop swelled at the end of a hair of the beard, shivering and bright. It detached itself and fell in a silver flash, striking a withered leaf with a sharp pat. (p. 220)

In representing the tears as "lights," Golding refuses to sentimentalize the creature's grief, and perhaps transfigures it.

In the concluding chapter of *The Inheritors,* Golding shifts his point of view once more, making us now look over the shoulder and into the mind of Tuami, the second-in-command of the new men. The shift has been prepared for by our technical separation from Lok in the pages that I have just considered, and it is of crucial importance to the meaning of *The Inheritors.* For, by linking us in this way with the new men, Golding forces us to take to ourselves, indeed roots in us, the cruelty and evil that Homo sapiens has displayed in his dealings with the Neanderthal people—the same cruelty and evil which Golding has dramatized so powerfully, earlier in the novel, through contrasting the two groups and allying us with the innocent victims. But there is a further point: to secure our identification of ourselves with the new men, Golding must make them appealing in their own right, despite the terrible things they have done. And to me the most astonishing fact about the concluding chapter is Golding's success in nourishing our sympathies for these beings.[5] He does not gloss over the behavior they have exhibited previously: the boat contains the weapons and liquor that we have seen before; Vivani is still self-conscious and vain; Tuami again feels lust when he looks at her and still sharpens a dagger for Marlan's heart; the killing of the Neanderthal people lives on in Tuami's mind, though he tries to justify the new men by saying, "If we had not we should have died" (p. 228) ; and the presence in the boat of Tanakil —who has been shocked by the eating of Liku, then lost her mind on being offered to propitiate Lok and Fa, and can now only utter, "Liku!"—is a continuing reminder to the new men and to us of their evil capacities.

But, without palliating these horrors, Golding tempers our response to the new men by showing us fully, for the first time, what it is like to be inside them and how they have been driven to act as they have. All the hints planted previously in the story—which I have listed earlier in my text— about their fears, sense of strain, weakness, confusion, and love for their own are realized now in the reflections of Tuami and the behavior of the others. (In the final representation of Lok, as we observed, Golding charged the recapitulated details by reporting them in a factual manner, from the perspective of a disengaged human being; in the closing chapter, the recapitulated details gain emotional power in a different way, through the alteration of vantage point that allows us to know more than we did, but here Golding does not employ a strategy of understatement.) Through a whole series of items, Golding encourages us to regard the new men as in many respects similar to the Neanderthal men with whom we have sympathized previously. The new men, too, have lost some members of their tribe in the engagements between the two groups. As the Neanderthal people have had their nightmares after the disappearance of Ha and the death of Mal, so the new men have had theirs as a result of meeting up with the people (pp. 183–84) , a nightmare that continues to possess the dislocated mind of Tanakil whether she sleeps or wakes (p. 226) . From the vantage point of Tuami, of course, it is the new men who are continually referred to as "the people"—by this point in the story the term is too loaded with emotion to operate merely ironically—while the Neanderthal men have become "forest devils." And, in the last chapter, the new men generally respond to the Neanderthal baby with the same mixture of attraction and repulsion that has defined the Neanderthal people's reaction to the new men: when Vivani nurses it, "The people were grinning at her too as if they felt the strange, tugging mouth, as if in spite of them there was a well of feeling opened in love and fear. They made adoring and submissive sounds, reached out their hands, and at the same time they shuddered . . . at the too-nimble feet and the red, curly hair" (p. 231). More surprising is the kinship with Lok that Tuami reveals, both in his weakness and in his confusion. Though he hates Marlan, he needs to turn to his chief for comfort as well as for stability (pp. 227–29). And he repeatedly betrays his confusion, intellectual—"He tried to perform a calculation in his aching head, tried to balance the current, the wind, the dug-out but he could come to no conclusion" (p. 224)—and moral: "I am like a pool, he thought, some tide has filled me, the sand is swirling, the waters are obscured and strange things are creeping out of the cracks and crannies in my mind" (p. 227). Clearly his self-awareness does put him on a moral plane rather different than Lok's; nevertheless, though Tuami constantly seeks to excuse the terrible deeds of the new men, he can acknowledge the evil of his world—and potentially, I think, of himself—in a way that ties him closely to us, however endearing we have found Lok's innocence:

> He had hoped for the light as for a return to sanity and the manhood that seemed to have left them; but here was

dawn—past dawn—and they were what they had been in
the gap, haunted, bedeviled, full of strange irrational grief
like himself, or emptied, collapsed, and helplessly asleep.
It seemed as though the portage of the boats . . . had
taken them on to a new level not only of land but of
experience and emotion. The world with the boat moving
so slowly at the centre was dark amid the light, was un-
tidy, hopeless, dirty. (pp. 224–25)

But Golding's most dramatic association of the new men
with the Neanderthal people and of Tuami with Lok in the
final chapter occurs in that brilliantly conceived and wonderfully ironic passage where Tuami—rebuked by the
mother of Tanakil for his part in offering the girl to "devils"
who "have given . . . back a changeling"—looks to Marlan
for support and sees a figure whose details duplicate the
details of the Neanderthal-like figures that the new men
themselves have drawn when making their offerings to the
"forest devils" (pp. 199, 215) :

> The sand was swirling in Tuami's brain. He thought in
> panic: they have given me back a changed Tuami; what
> shall I do? Only Marlan is the same—smaller, weaker but
> the same. He peered forrard to find the changeless one as
> something he could hold on to. The sun was blazing on
> the red sail and Marlan was red. His arms and legs were
> contracted, his hair stood out and his beard, his teeth were
> wolf's teeth and his eyes like blind stones. The mouth was
> opening and shutting.
> "They cannot follow us, I tell you. They cannot pass
> over water." (p. 229)

In his confusion and "panic," Tuami again resembles Lok
(for instance, the Lok who, feeling strangely changed and

cut off when he follows the track of the new men, needs to reestablish his identity through mingling with his own kind) . He is like Lok, too, in apparently not grasping the significance of what he sees, just as Lok has "never seen any thing like" the figure he observes (p. 199) —although, ironically, Lok later thinks of the figure as "some kind of man" (p. 215) . But for us, the significance and irony of the present passage are overwhelmingly plain: it makes of Marlan—and the statement is morally true of Homo sapiens—the monstrous and evil creature that the new men have imagined Neanderthal man to be. And there is a further irony in the very limitation of the new men here, though their ignorance itself may also draw us to them: Tuami yearns toward "the changeless one" but finds a Marlan temporarily transformed; Marlan declares that the forest devils "cannot follow us," yet he himself has just been represented as one, and of course the new men are bearing away with them the baby of the devils.

The significance of this passage and its ironies prepare us to understand at last the full sense of Golding's title. For it is only a part of the truth that the title supplies a simple ironic commentary on Homo sapiens, who has exhibited anything but the meekness requisite for inheriting the earth. The new men are indeed inheritors, inheritors of their terrifying experience with the Neanderthal people. The experience persists in the continuing fears of them all, in their ambiguous reactions to the baby they take with them, in the reality of the mad Tanakil's possession by the memory of Liku—even in that vision of Marlan, though Tuami does not comprehend the fact, which links the chief with Neanderthal man. And the fundamental irony is that the new men have generated this experience out of themselves, have been driven by their fears and cruelty to re-create the Neanderthal people in their own inhuman—or all-too-human—image. Surely

Tuami's repeated mention of the change which his people have passed through in their exposure to the Neanderthal tribe is Golding's way of suggesting that the new men have themselves undergone a Fall of sorts in the course of the novel:

> Tuami, his head full of swirling sand, tried to think of the time when the devil [the baby] would be full grown. In this upland country, safe from pursuit . . . but shut off from men by the devil-haunted mountains, what sacrifice would they be forced to perform to a world of confusion? They were as different from the group of bold hunters and magicians who had sailed up the river . . . as a soaked feather is from a dry one. Restlessly he turned the ivory in his hands. What was the use of sharpening it against a man? Who would sharpen a point against the darkness of the world? (p. 231)

But their fall, unlike the fall in which we have seen Lok and Fa involved, is engendered by themselves.[6]

In what I have said about the guilt of the new men, I do not wish to minimize their human appeal in these final pages, an appeal I have been trying to stress. In fact, their guilt itself probably helps us to identify ourselves with them. But, as in the case of our last view of Lok, Golding refuses to sentimentalize the new men. To be sure, Tuami stops sharpening the ivory; the new men shriek with laughter at the antics of the Neanderthal baby; and Tuami can sense, in the juxtaposition of the baby's "rump" and Vivani's "head," that the two things somehow go together "and made a shape you could feel with your hands. They were waiting in the rough ivory of the knife-haft that was so much more important than the blade. They were an answer . . ." (p. 233). But this "answer" retains all the ambiguities of the new men: the "rump" strikes them as "ridiculous" yet "intimidating," and the "love of the woman" is both "frightened" and "angry." All through the chapter, any lingering manifestation of the Neanderthal people has called forth the terrors of the new men: even the sound of the falling ice that signals to us the entombing of Lok leaves Marlan "crouched, making stabbing motions at the mountains with his fingers, and his eyes were glaring like stones" (p. 232). For us, the last speech in the novel—Marlan's reassurance to his people that they are safe because the Neanderthal men "live in the darkness under the trees" (p. 233)—is shot through with irony, not only because they have the baby with them, but because we have already heard Tuami speculate that they may be compelled to offer some "sacrifice" in the future "to a world of confusion." And in the last words of the book, Tuami looks towards the shore to which the new men must sometime come, and "he could not see if the line of darkness had an ending" (p. 233). It is the triumph of *The Inheritors* that Golding, after so highlighting the qualities of Homo sapiens by exhibiting him to us via the perspective of Neanderthal man, yet compels us finally to take these new men to ourselves in all their unpleasantness and so to experience once more what we are as human beings.

1. I shall give page references to *The Inheritors,* A Harvest Book (New York, 1962).

2. It is a critical commonplace that, in *The Inheritors,* Golding reverses the attitudes towards Neanderthal man and Homo sapiens expressed by H. G. Wells in *The Outline of History,* just as *Lord of the Flies* reverses the thesis of Ballantyne's *The Coral Island.* To my knowledge, Peter Green was the first to point out—in "The World of William Golding," reprinted in *A Source Book,* pp. 170–89—the rela-

tionship between Golding's novel and a story by Wells called "The Grisly Folk," which also records the encountering of Neanderthal man by Homo sapiens and contains several details that Golding reshapes to his own purposes in his book.

3. While we know Lok more intimately than anyone else because we see so much of what happens along with him, Fa is the most rounded character among the rest of the Neanderthal people and displays an appealing sympathy herself. It is true that she dominates the less imaginative Lok after the death of Mal, superintending, among other things, their crossing of the river to reconnoiter the island: even in this incident, however, she is humanized by her terror of the water (she makes Lok go on the log first), though she later brags that she has not made the noise he did in his fear (p. 125). Golding emphasizes the intensity of her love for the baby by her reaction on discovering that Vivani has milk in her breasts to feed the captured new one, for Fa simultaneously laughs and weeps, overjoyed that the baby will not starve even while she grieves—"as though she were bearing the pain of a long thorn in her side" (p. 152)—for the loss of the child. The most dramatic instance of Fa's sympathy for Lok is her concealing of Liku's death, a decision that turns out, ironically, to be as big a blunder as anything Lok does in their inept efforts to rescue their own from the new men.

4. Although Frank Kermode is one of Golding's strongest supporters and most intelligent critics (see "The Novels of William Golding," reprinted in *A Source Book*, pp. 107–20) he seems to me off target, if I read him correctly, when he writes of *The Inheritors*, "And at the end we abruptly leave Lok; suddenly, with a loss of sympathy, observe him with our normal sight, joining the new men, our own sort" (p. 115). If he feels a "loss of sympathy" for Lok in the pages under discussion, as opposed to the final chapter of the novel, I think their actual effect quite the reverse, a heightening of sympathy.

5. James Gindin finds that in this last chapter the "theme does not change," that "the 'gimmick,' the switch in point of view, merely repeats what the rest of the novel has already demonstrated" and so "breaks the unity" of the book "without adding relevant perspective" (*A Source Book*, p. 135). I suppose one might argue that the closing chapter provides no new intellectual perspective on the book's theme, but certainly it engages us in a new emotional perspective and thus proves the theme, as it were, on our pulses. James Baker, in his discussion of *The Inheritors*, appears often to aim at qualifying the contrast between the Neanderthal people and the new men; but, when he sums up the effect of the whole book, he seems to me to overlook the

full working of the last chapter and to insist that the contrast between the two groups is unqualified: "We find in *The Inheritors* the traits of each species frozen in a radical contrast which sustains the allegory but threatens the illusion of reality" (p. 29). Bernard Oldsey and Stanley Weintraub—in *The Art of William Golding* (New York, 1965) —sense what is going on in the final chapter, for they declare that "it accomplishes in respect to the life and problems of Tuami's tribe what the first two hundred-odd pages do for Lok's tribe" and refer later to "a dualistically sympathetic reading of the novel" (pp. 65, 69). But I cannot discover in their summaries precisely how the last chapter operates to affect the reader. And I find their suggestion that the story is somehow about "the artist" and their talk about the "point" of the novel very confusing (pp. 68–70) —as confusing as their suggestion of Conrad and Hueffer's *Inheritors* as some kind of source for Golding's book, or their statement that *"The Inheritors* is a subtle dramatization of the very technique by which the novel is accomplished. Golding here stands as something of an overseer, the reader as inter-seer, Tuami a medial-seer, and Lok, the father of us all, a base-seer" (p. 70).

6. Peter Green has pointed out that the fall of Lok and Fa is a "blazingly heretical version of the Paradisal legend," that "it is Man himself whom Golding identifies with the Serpent, and who tempts Lok to eat of the Tree of Knowledge" (*A Source Book*, p. 180). But he does not add explicitly that, according to the indication of the novel, Homo sapiens has also accomplished his own fall, though Green does insist that in this book "it is humanity, and humanity alone, that generates evil" (p. 178).

III

Pincher Martin

Many critics have found William Golding's third novel, *Pincher Martin* (1956), his most challenging book, and a few have praised it in the highest—perhaps extravagant—terms. Frank Kermode describes it as "a wonderful achievement" in which "There is no distinguishing . . . between a compassion that might be called religious and the skill of an artist," and he goes on, "Yeats spoke of an intellectual construct which enables him to 'hold in a single thought reality and justice'; *Pincher Martin* is such a thought" (*A Source Book*, pp. 117–18). John Peter writes that "The book seems to me, in all seriousness, as brilliant a conception as any fable in English prose," and that it moves beyond Golding's earlier novels in being "richer because exploratory, a configuration of symbols rather than an allegory," a symbolic structure whose "meaning is difficult to exhaust" (*A Source Book*, p. 32). Certainly *Pincher Martin* is Golding's most problematic novel for anyone who is interested in literature's effects upon the reader or for anyone who puzzles about the status of the represented reality in a literary work; and the book's texture—especially once we come to sense what is going on in the story—is more dense than that of any other novel by Golding, makes more sustained demands on the reader's awareness.

These difficulties originate in the extraordinary fiction that Golding has imagined for this novel. Through most of its pages, we seem to watch a man from a torpedoed ship struggle by himself to survive on a rock in the North Atlantic and also show himself, through his recollections, to be a singularly unpleasant person. But the final sentence of the novel—and the ending made the book something of a *cause célèbre* soon after publication—reveals unequivocally that this person, Pincher Martin, has in fact been dead since almost the start of the story, that what we have really been watching is a man driven by his ego to spin a world and an existence out of himself in a desperate attempt to evade the death which has occurred. Some critics, viewing *Pincher Martin* as analogous to Ambrose Bierce's "An Occurrence at Owl Creek Bridge," understand the novel as an expansion of the few seconds just prior to Martin's death by drowning. Yet such a reading strikes me as motivated by a wish to explain the book in commonsensical terms, and in effect denies Golding's adventurousness in imagining a story about a dead person. The interpretation weakens the power of Martin's ego, and it also seems to me to run against the grain of the novel, for we are constantly made to feel that Martin seeks to avoid acknowledging something that has already happened. Other critics, myself included, take Martin as dead—the title of the book as originally published in America was *The Two Deaths of Christopher Martin*—and the commentary by Golding himself on his novel indicates that such is the case. His remarks are so generally helpful an introduction to the story as to be worth reproducing at length:

> Christopher Hadley Martin had no belief in anything but the importance of his own life: no love, no God. Because he was created in the image of God he had a freedom of choice which he used to centre the world on himself. He did not believe in purgatory and therefore when he died it was not presented to him in overtly theological terms. The greed for life which had been the mainspring of his nature, forced him to refuse the selfless act of dying. He continued to exist separately in a world composed of his own murderous nature. His drowned body lies rolling in the Atlantic but the ravenous ego invents a rock for him to endure on. It is the memory of an aching tooth. Ostensi-

bly and rationally he is a survivor from a torpedoed destroyer: but deep down he knows the truth. He is not
fighting for bodily survival but for his continuing identity
in the face of what will smash it and sweep it away—the
black lightning, the compassion of God. For Christopher,
the Christ-bearer, has become Pincher Martin who is little
but greed. Just to be Pincher is purgatory; to be Pincher
for eternity is hell.[1]

Whatever his sense of Martin's condition, every reader
feels unsettled to some degree by Golding's conclusion, I
suspect, because the world created by Martin through most
of the novel has seemed so compelling actual. And for many
readers, the matter of their response is further complicated
by the fact that Martin's extraordinary struggle to endure, as
it originally unfolds in the book, affects them as heroic
despite the nastiness that he also exhibits, despite the moral
evaluation of him insisted upon by the book as a whole.
Margaret Walters expresses this position very forcefully:

> . . . the dominant imaginative impression the book
> makes upon us is neither the inadequacy of man's per-
> sonal resources to achieve salvation, nor the ignobility of
> his preoccupation with his own small existence. We feel,
> rather, the resource and courage—the vitality—in Mar-
> tin's fight for life, even as we recognize his egoism; in
> fact the egoism, which the book claims damns him,
> emerges as a necessary condition of that vitality. Such a
> struggle for life cannot, I think, serve as an image of
> damnation and spiritual death; it suggests possibilities
> and moral complexities that the author's thesis, the con-
> trolling pattern, fails to comprehend. (*A Source Book,* pp.
> 102–3)

Such a response to the novel, even when one does not share it, can hardly be quarreled with profitably.

And perhaps another issue that hardly admits of an answer satisfactory to all is the status as reality of the world that Pincher Martin imagines for himself in much of the story. Certainly that world strikes us as undeniably real: because of Martin's behavior, which is rendered in such convincing detail; because he is presented to us in the third person, the reporting of an omniscient author thus vouching, as it were, for the actuality of what goes on; and because of our normal expectations as readers of fiction, which Golding does little immediately to allay. (In spite of the author's claims about falling over backwards to make the novel clear, he could scarcely afford to represent Martin's death unambiguously on the book's second page, for I should think many readers unlikely to go on with a story about a dead person: Martin's struggle to survive will seem most dramatically convincing, most "real," if we believe him to be alive.) Yet by the end of the book we must regard what has happened to Martin as the projection of a dead man's mind—and to what order of reality do we assign that projection? This shift in levels of reality, and the consequently fluid relation of the reader to the events of the story, may tempt us to think briefly of *The Counterfeiters* in relation to Golding's book, Gide playing even more complicated games with different levels of reality too numerous for me to sort out here. But *The Counterfeiters* does not sustain so apparently uncomplicated a version of a conventionally substantial world as does *Pincher Martin* in its first chapters (though I might add that Gide's novel affects me finally, for all its deliberate violations of our sense of what is real in fiction, as offering us an illusion of actuality convincing because of its very inclusiveness). Even if we grant Golding the license as a writer of fiction to make a "real" world out of a dead man's thoughts, what is the ontological status of those lapses into nothingness, into non-being, that occur—if that is the word—when Martin experiences his fits? I suppose we must take them as somehow akin to the intrusions of something other on Martin's ego that crop up periodically in the novel (such as the appearance of God near the story's end) —though nothingness seems to me to pose a special problem to our comprehension in the fiction that Golding has invented here.

As for the difficulties that reside in the dense texture of Golding's prose itself in this novel, most of them admit of solution, at least on a second or third reading of the book, when our knowledge of Martin's death has prepared us to understand why he flinches from certain thoughts and why his mind moves as evasively at moments as it does, even while his ego creates that astonishingly substantial world of rock and day-to-day suffering that so dominates one's initial impression of *Pincher Martin*. The texture of Golding's prose I shall illustrate later on in this chapter, through exploring a rather long passage in which Martin ostensibly endures a fever. But first I want to separate several narrative threads that are woven together in the finished novel and glance at one typically oblique sequence of events; then I shall comment on the series of flashbacks that constitute one of the novel's structures. Finally, after treating the long passage just mentioned, I shall take up the ending of *Pincher Martin* and argue for its relevance to Golding's meaning.

To the person first reading *Pincher Martin,* the novel appears to record the desperate struggle for survival of a man after the destroyer on which he served as an officer has been torpedoed. Golding takes us through this struggle inch by inch: the locale and events of the story are narrowly limited, and he subjects us to so sustained a close-up of the man's experience that physical details seem to register on our muscles and even minor decisions by Martin are fraught with consequences. Blown off his ship, Martin manages to get to a rock that suddenly looms up in the mist, scales a small cliff by using limpets to help him up, and takes shelter under a slab of stone. Gradually he pulls himself together to explore the rock: discovering a pool of water he can drink, building a pile of stones which he calls "the dwarf" as a signal for rescue, and forcing himself to eat anemones and mussels. His reconstitution of himself seems complete when he verifies his existence through his identification disc— "Christopher Hadley Martin. Martin. Chris. I am what I always was!"—and goes confidently on to "survey the estate" of the island.[2] Yet the strain on him increases in spite of his efforts to impose patterns of his own upon the rock: after all his labor over the dwarf, he suddenly realizes that he should have made a sign recognizable by planes rather than by surface vessels; but his strength and will to finish the job give out before he has completed an effective signal by piling seaweed in a line, just as they give out before he has completed the Claudian, the cuttings in the rock by which he plans to add to his supply of water. Through the last third of the novel, Martin appears to disintegrate slowly. He suffers first from what appears to be a fever, and his thoughts become more and more like the hallucinations of a man under tremendous pressure. Just when it seems to him that he has recovered himself physically by a self-administered enema which purges him of the harsh food he has eaten, he falls into a fit—and then must strive harder than ever to re-create the self out of its shattered remnants: "Something was coming up to the surface. It was uncertain of its identity because it had forgotten its name. It was disorganized in pieces. It struggled to get these pieces together because then it would know what it was. There was a rhythmical noise and disconnection. The pieces came shakily together and he was lying sideways on the rock and a snoring noise was coming from his mouth" (p. 167). Martin clings to his sanity for a time, though apparently on the verge of madness. But a terrible storm sweeps over the rock during which he first challenges the elements, next challenges a manifestation of God Himself, then destroys his own supply of water, and finally broods—reduced to a pair of red claws—as the "black lightning" obliterates his world. In the concluding chapter, Golding shifts us to an island in the Hebrides where Martin's body has washed ashore; and the naval officer who has come to identify the body assures his listener, in the last sentence of the novel, that the drowned man could not have suffered because "He didn't even have time to kick off his seaboots" (p. 208)—the act that we apparently witnessed Martin performing on the fourth page of the story.

So much for the ostensible narrative of Pincher Martin. But even the surface of the story is more difficult than I have just suggested, the play of Martin's consciousness developing in rather complicated ways which I want now to indicate. In the novel's first paragraphs, when Martin is about to drown, Golding dramatizes his physical existence as quite literally elemental, a struggle for air among water that burns or feels like "stones" and "gravel." I quote a passage to show how concretely Golding renders Martin's situation:

When the air had gone with the shriek, water came in to fill its place—burning water, hard in the throat and mouth as stones that hurt. He hutched his body towards the place where air had been but now it was gone and there was nothing but black, choking welter. His body let

loose its panic and his mouth strained open till the hinges
of his jaw hurt. Water thrust in, down, without mercy. Air
came with it for a moment so that he fought in what
might have been the right direction. But the water re-
claimed him and spun so that knowledge of where the air
might be was erased completely. Turbines were screaming
in his ears and green sparks [the machinery of his nervous
system] flew out from the centre like tracer. There was a
piston engine too [his heart], racing out of gear and making the whole universe shake. Then for a moment there
was air like a cold mask against his face and he bit into it.
Air and water mixed, dragged down into his body like
gravel. (p. 7)

In this paragraph, "knowledge"—"of where the air might
be"—is wiped out, yet Martin gathers himself for one last
scream, "Moth—," which is cut off in the middle. And Golding goes on: "But the man lay suspended behind the whole
commotion, detached from his jerking body. . . . Could . . .
a face have been fashioned to fit the attitude of his consciousness . . . that face would have worn a snarl. But the real jaw
was contorted down and distant, the mouth was slopped full.
. . . There was no face but there was a snarl" (p. 8). Disre-
garding his physical death, Martin's consciousness persists,
focuses on a "picture" out of the past—significantly, a picture of "a little world . . . which one could control" (p.
8) —and advances via mental associations with this picture
to a "realization of the lifebelt" which supposedly supports
him; as a result of this "realization," "a flood of connected
images came back" (p. 9), and Martin's consciousness has in
effect reconstituted him: "Suddenly he knew who he was and
where he was" (p. 10).
    After he reaches the island, he is further revived by an-

other thought, "valuable . . . because it gave him back a bit of his personality":

"I should be about as heavy as this on Jupiter."
At once he was master. (p. 27)

But behind Martin's rationality, though often informing his thoughts through the first part of the story, lurks a more powerful force, what comes to be called the "dark centre," his ego: "There was at the centre of all the pictures and pains and voices a fact like a bar of steel, a thing—that which was so nakedly the centre of everything that it could not even examine itself. In the darkness of the skull, it existed, a darker dark, self-existent and indestructible" (p. 45). It is this ego that compels him to resist admitting the first fit he suffers or to hold out when—in a passage reminiscent of Simon's confrontations with the pig's head in *Lord of the Flies*, though Simon's motives are the reverse of Martin's —the "chill and the exhaustion" that he experiences on the rock tempt him to "Give up. Leave go" (p. 45). And it is the ego that gains its happiest triumph when he has clutched and read his identification disc, which assures him briefly that he exists ordinarily in a real world: "All at once it seemed to him that he came out of his curious isolation inside the globe of his head and was extended normally through his limbs. He lived again on the surface of his eyes, he was out in the air. Daylight crowded down on him, sunlight, there was a sparkle on the sea. The solid rock was coherent as an object. . . . It was a position in a finite sea at the intersection of two lines, there were real ships passing under the horizon" (pp. 76–77).

For a time Martin's ego, assisted off and on by his reason, operates fairly successfully to sustain the illusion of his physical existence. The mind works out a series of determinedly rational points to govern behavior on the rock. When the body undergoes a fever, the ego may veer towards an admission of the death that has happened, but the mind—now associated with what the mouth utters—chirps on to explain everything in terms of "sexual images" (p. 146). And when the ego is frightened by its intuition of "a pattern emerging" from all of Martin's past—a pattern that acknowledges the presence of something other, something alien to the self, in the universe—the ego defends itself momentarily on the grounds that patterns are created only by one's intellect acting on its own: "Education, a key to all patterns, itself able to impose them, to create" (p. 163).

But rationality, at least in any ordinary form, proves an insufficient support for Martin's world, especially after he has suffered his second fit, knows himself to have lapsed temporarily into a nothingness that belies everything which his self has struggled to create. Through the last part of the novel, both the mind and the ego in their separate ways periodically take refuge in pretending to madness, for madness does anyway predicate existence; but their efforts are doomed to failure. Initially, they can accommodate the vision of "the old woman" on the rock—an image of otherness out of Martin's past—by identifying her with "the Dwarf," the pile of stones that Martin has built (p. 176). And the first touch of the black lightning that later dissolves Martin's world is normalized by the rational mouth as mere "Lightning," though the "centre" then "made the mouth work deliberately" to utter "Black lightning," perhaps because even to formulate the phrase is to control the phenomenon to some extent (p. 177). This flaw in their universe immediately drives the mouth and the center to embark on the role

of Shakespeare's "Poor Tom," but the degree of madness
that Edgar represents is not enough to protect the center.
The mouth may try to assert that the rock is real and the
creature on it mad: ". . . Who could invent all that com-
plication of water, running true to form, obeying the laws
of nature to the last drop? And of course a human brain must
turn in time and the universe be muddled. But beyond the
muddle there will still be actuality and a poor mad creature
clinging to a rock in the middle of the sea" (p. 180). Yet the
ego knows better: "There is no centre of sanity in madness.
Nothing like this 'I' sitting in here, staving off the time that
must come. The last repeat of the pattern. Then the black
lightning" (p. 181). Nevertheless, the self continues attempting to evade the truth, later allowing the mouth to demonstrate logically the madness of them both as it addresses the
center: "You are the intersections of all the currents. You do
not exist apart from me. If I have gone mad then you have
gone mad. You are speaking, in there, you and I are one and
mad" (p. 191). But when they work together to "Be a naked
madman on a rock" by slashing to death the vision of the old
woman, "They knew the blood was sea water and the cold,
crumpling flesh that was ripped and torn nothing but oil-
skin" (p. 193). Climactically, they seek to arm themselves
against the manifestation of God by arguing that "hallucina-
tion" is what "a madman" can "expect" on a "real rock," by
insisting that He is "a projection" of Martin's "mind" (p.
194), by declaring to the figure—in words through which the
self interweaves a pretense of madness with the sheerest
egotism—that "On the sixth day he created God. Therefore
I permit you to use nothing but my own vocabulary. In his
own image created he Him" (p. 196).[3] But the black lightning comes on all the same, though the center tries at last to

prove its madness by breaking up the pool in which it has hoarded water, and Martin's universe disintegrates into nothingness.

The third narrative strand that I want to isolate in the novel is the series of fractures in Martin's world which hint, more or less obliquely, at the fact of his death. In a general way, Golding's phrasing itself often suggests Martin's condition. His pains are recurrently described as fiery: "a burning without heat" (p. 24) ; "fires . . . flaring and spitting in his flesh" (p. 55) ; "their distant fires, their slow burnings, their racks and pincers were at least far enough away" (p. 49). This imagery, indicative of a hell of sorts, finds an ironic echo in such statements by Martin as "I'm damned if I'll die" (p. 72) or "I went through hell in the sea" (p. 122). At moments, Martin views himself as "Like a dead man" (p. 34), feels the flying seagulls to tell him "that he was far better dead, floating in the sea like a burst hammock" (p. 56), and searches "for hope in his mind but the warmth had gone or if he found anything it was an intellectual and bloodless ghost" (p. 117). But of course we are inclined to take all such expressions as figurative rather than literal on first reading the book. And Golding renders the violations of Martin's universe, so substantial a projection of Martin's ego, with a similar indirection that makes them easy to overlook.

I shall not rehearse all these violations, but simply indicate some of the items that turn up several times, acquiring added significance on each appearance, and cite a brief sequence of charged reactions on the part of Martin. One of the important items repeatedly referred to is a "tooth": alluded to first in a simile (p. 24), the tooth—which Martin has lost years earlier—is gradually revealed as the model for the rock that he has invented to prolong existence. Golding's second mention of a tooth will show how ambiguously he handles such references:

> "Where the hell am I?"
> A single point of rock, peak of a mountain range, one tooth set in the ancient jaw of a sunken world . . . and how many miles from dry land? An evil pervasion . . . a deep and generalized terror set him clawing at the rock with his blunt fingers. (p. 30)

In this context, early in the novel, the "tooth" seems simply a way of describing a real rock; and Martin's "evil pervasion" and "generalized terror" seem a reaction normal enough to a living survivor of a ship that has been sunk, rather than the response of Martin's ego to a dimly intuited fact it resists recognizing. In the same way, the pressures of Martin's apparent situation disguise his first fit, that gap in his existence which so terrifies him when he later comes to acknowledge what has happened. As his reaction is initially represented by Golding, the major hint that something untoward has transpired is Martin's notice of the "white water" in which his face has been lying and the "too-smooth wetness" on his cheek (p. 42) —details which are not explained for over one hundred pages, when the "dark centre" remembers that "Guano is insoluble" and so that the white stuff must have been produced by the fit rather than the gulls (p. 174). A third critical item is the lobster that Martin seems to perceive in the seaweed about the island: "At once, as if his eye had created it, he saw the lobster among the weed, different in dragon-shape, different in colour" (p. 111). But, unless we are reading very carefully, we will realize neither the force of the dependent clause nor the false color of the living lobster until the impossibility of a red lobster swimming in the sea dawns on Martin himself (p. 167).

A fairly characteristic sequence of hints about Martin's real condition occurs in a passage after he has climbed down the rock to collect seaweed and happens on a stone that he recalls having tried to move earlier but that "wouldn't move although it was cracked." As he looks at the stone now, however, "the crack was wider. The whole stone had moved and skewed perhaps an eighth of an inch. Inside the crack was a terrible darkness" (p. 124). Maybe the "terrible darkness" foreshadows the black lightning that wipes out the rock later on; anyway, this violation of the remembered details, whatever its cause, unnerves Martin to the extent that he starts "envisaging the whole rock as a thing in the water" and brooding on its familiarity (pp. 124–25). No overt reference to the tooth is made in the paragraph during which Martin gropes for the source of the rock's familiarity to him: the closest he comes is in recollecting "the rocks of childhood . . . remembered in the darkness of bed . . . imagined as a shape one's fingers can feel in the air—" (p. 125). Farther along on the same page,

> He put his hands on either cheek to think but the touch of hair distracted him.
> "I must have a beard pretty well. Bristles, anyway. Strange that bristles go on growing even when the rest of you is—"

But he catches himself on the verge of uttering "dead" and tries to ignore his situation by gathering a load of seaweed.

Through the last part of the book, the flaws in the logic of Martin's world assail his awareness more and more insistently, his realization that he could not have seen a red lobster in the sea, for example, bringing on his second fit immediately, which in turn leads him to recognize that he has manufactured the rock out of the memory of a tooth. As his world dissolves, his consciousness is increasingly invaded by indications of otherness in the universe, an otherness that itself denies the postulate of Martin's private universe, the total self-sufficiency of the ego. Thus his memory of a nightmarish childhood compulsion, to go down into the cellar for some portentous confrontation, keeps infringing on Martin's consciousness until he finally relives the experience:

> Darkness in the corner doubly dark, thing looming, feet tied, near, an unknown looming, an opening darkness, the heart and being of all imaginable terror. Pattern repeated from the beginning of time, approach of the unknown thing, a dark centre that turned its back on the thing that created it and struggled to escape. (p. 179)

Whatever its precise contours, "the unknown thing" evidently has its source in something other than Martin's ego, while the fact that it "created" Martin's "dark centre" implies that "the thing" is to be associated with God.[4] And, as the reference to its repetition suggests, the "Pattern" applies even on the rock, connecting Martin's past with his present and confirming the impossibility of his shielding himself ultimately against the otherness, whether it manifests itself as the image of God which he later sees or as the black lightning which at last "erased like an error" the world that Martin has invented (p. 201).

One component in the story of *Pincher Martin* I have hardly touched on yet, the series of flashbacks spaced through the novel to show us Martin's earlier life as a civilian and as a naval officer. The flashbacks are important in various ways, but also the least satisfying sections of the book, to my mind, and I want now to consider them briefly. One important point easy to overlook is that they, too, are projections of Martin's consciousness. He does not really sleep on the rock because, as he once admits, "sleep was a consenting to die, to go into complete unconsciousness, the personality defeated" (p. 91) ; while he seems to rest, then, his ego sustains itself, warding off nothingness through remembering the past. These memories also serve the story through developing a narrative thread of their own in the gradual revelation of how Martin has acted toward his best, indeed only, friend, Nathaniel Walterson. Even in Martin's first jumbled recollections, when he struggles in the water or after he has landed on the island, an order that he has given isolates itself in his mind, presumably the right order for his ship to avoid the torpedo that has sunk her. Through later flashbacks, we become aware of how sensitive he is on the score of Nat and learn that Martin has contemplated killing his friend—by having the ship change course unexpectedly and thus causing Nat to topple into the sea as he prays by the railing—because Nat has married the one girl to reject Martin's advances. But only in the last of the flashbacks do we discover that Martin has given the order he did, not to avoid a torpedo, but to murder Nat (pp. 185–86) .[5] The chief office of the flashbacks, however, is to make clear how nastily egocentric Martin is, and they reveal his essential nature more directly than do his actions on the rock. His vanity, his unremitting exploitation of everyone else in his determination to get on, his greedy indulgence of every appetite are emphasized again and again. To cite two examples of his behavior: although he has been forced into military service because the director of the plays in which he appears will not declare his work essential (pp. 153–54), he acts the role of the humble patriot when asked why he joined the Navy and wishes to become an officer, talking glibly of his desire to "help" and his hope of "hitting the old Hun for six" (p. 94). This charade juxtaposes him absolutely to Nat, who, though conscientiously objecting to war, nevertheless feels that "the responsibility of deciding" not to serve "is too much for one man" (p. 155). A sharper commentary on Martin is provided by the first detailed recollection of Mary that he allows himself, rather late in the novel (pp. 147–53). She is the girl whom Nat has married, but who so lives for Martin because she is the only person to violate his ego: for she has rebuffed his advances, and when in effect raped by him (though Martin has tossed in a promise of marriage which he quickly retracts once he has gotten what he wants), she cries, her "real tears" convincing even Martin of how enduringly she hates him.

The relevance of the flashbacks to illuminating Martin's character is plain. But, perhaps because Golding's plan for the novel forbids him to develop them at length, or because the world of sea and rock that he creates is so substantial, the life and characters represented in the flashbacks seem to me relatively wan: asserted rather than dramatically compelling. The passage in which Martin's colleagues in the theater discuss his casting as one of the Seven Deadly Sins, for instance, strikes me as somewhat labored and over-explicit (pp. 118–20). The triangular relationship involving Martin, Nat, and Mary appears to me too pat in its execution, especially when the innocent Nat insists that Martin be his best man and Martin uncharacteristically shows, for the only time in the novel, some trace of conscience in warning Nat against Martin himself (p. 158). It is difficult for me to

imagine that a person like Martin would anyway feel affection for someone like Nat. But, leaving that objection aside,
and granting that Nat's religious interests may entitle him to
speak as he does early in the novel of "black lightning" and
"the technique of dying," his statements about Martin's "extraordinary capacity to endure" and his declaration that
Martin will die within a few years seem to me frightfully
arbitrary (pp. 70–71) —as arbitrary, and unnecessary, as Simon's prediction in *Lord of the Flies* about Ralph's ultimate
survival.

Although I have been complaining that the quality of life
and character rendered by Golding in the flashbacks themselves of *Pincher Martin* is relatively thin, the life of Martin's consciousness, as he fights to sustain the illusion of his
existence on the rock, is densely imagined and can be exceed-
ingly complicated. In outlining the narrative progress of the
novel, I have indicated that Martin splits up into a pain-
wracked body, a mouth that clings to the rational, and a
dark center that strives to ignore the death which has happened; and these three elements interact in the rather long
passage which I shall examine. It will be clear at a glance
how much the passage differs from, say, Golding's dramatization of a typical reaction by Lok in *The Inheritors*. There,
Lok's sensuous response to the physical details of the external world counted for almost everything and the activity of
his mind for very little. But, though physical details from an
apparently real external world crop up repeatedly in the
passage to follow, the whole experience seems an hallucina-
tion of Martin's mind, and to interpret the experience we
must puzzle out the associative patterns of his private consciousness. Ostensibly, he is suffering from a fever, brought
on by something he has eaten, as he lies in the crevice of

stone that shelters him on the island. Actually, as I read the passage, the movement of his thoughts brings him close to reliving his drowning and thus to being confronted with the fact of his death, though the ego finally resists this knowledge again. Such is the drama that I shall try to sketch, though the passage is too charged with significant details for me to pretend to gloss it fully and so long that I must break it into segments (pp. 143–46).

Two bits of information by way of a prelude to the first section: the "tin box" is from an anecdote applied to Martin by one of his colleagues in the theater, the box containing one huge maggot that has fed on all the others but will itself be finally eaten; and the persons named toward the close of the section have all been exploited by Martin.

> The crevice enlarged and became populous. There were times when it was larger than the rock, larger than the world, times when it was a tin box so huge that a spade knocking at the side sounded like distant thunder. Then after that there was a time when he was back in rock and distant thunder was sounding like the knocking of a spade against a vast tin box. All the time the opening beneath his window [the rational mouth beneath his eyes] was dribbling on like the Forces Programme, cross-talking and singing to people whom he could not see but knew were there. For a moment or two he was home and his father was like a mountain. The thunder and lightning were playing round the mountain's head and his mother was weeping tears like acid and knitting a sock without a beginning or end. The tears were a kind of charm for after he had felt them scald him they changed the crevice into a pattern.
>
> The opening spoke.

"She is sorry for me on this rock."
Sybil was weeping and Alfred. Helen was crying. A
bright boy face was crying. He saw half-forgotten but now
clearly remembered faces and they were all weeping.
"That is because they know I am alone on a rock in the
middle of a tin box."

A delirium appropriate to fever is suggested by the reversal
and yet repetition of the second sentence in the third. But
the encompassing reality in the second sentence is the "tin
box," which is only a couple of steps away, for Martin, from
a confirmation of his death; by the third sentence, this reality has become something much safer for him, a real rock
and storm. The mouth goes "dribbling on like the Forces
Programme" to evade actuality, but the ego has further
resources of its own. Thus what seems a remembered quarrel
between his parents about Martin gets transformed, I would
guess, into a mythological tableau replete with security,
where an angry Zeus does not interfere with a Fate working
on an endless lifeline ("knitting a sock without a beginning
or end"). More important, the physical sweat presumably
starting in Martin because of the fever is translated by his
ego into "tears"—"tears" that "changed the crevice into a
pattern" both because, as sweat, they promise Martin that he
is alive and because, as tears, they minister to his self-pity by
assuring him that the whole world weeps for him. By his last
statement he is still holding to the notion of a rock, though
the reality of the "tin box," of his death, is threatening
again.
He continues to stave off the truth in the next segment,
though his ego is nearly put to rout. On one level, the
paragraph records Martin's fantasies as he lies in the crevice,

looking at the stone about him and becoming enveloped by his own sweat:

They wept tears that turned them to stone faces in a wall, masks hung in rows in a corridor without beginning or end. There were notices that said No Smoking, Gentlemen, Ladies, Exit and there were many uniformed attendants. Down there was the other room, to be avoided, because there the gods sat behind their terrible knees and feet of black stone, but here the stone faces wept and had wept. Their stone cheeks were furrowed, they were blurred and only recognizable by some indefinite mode of identity. Their tears made a pool on the stone floor so that his feet were burned to the ankles. He scrabbled to climb up the wall and the scalding stuff welled up his ankles to his calves, his knees. He was struggling, half-swimming, half-climbing. The wall was turning over, curving like the wall of a tunnel in the underground. The tears were no longer running down the stone to join the burning sea. They were falling freely, dropping on him. One came, a dot, a pearl, a ball, a globe, that moved on him, spread. He began to scream. He was inside the ball of water that was burning him to the bone and past. It consumed him utterly. He was dissolved and spread throughout the tear an extension of sheer, disembodied pain.

At first the ego still converts the sweat into "tears" of the world's pity (Martin seems to imagine the "tears" being shed endlessly for him, given the faint allusion to Niobe in "stone faces," and thus endlessly guaranteeing his existence). Then his attention swings back, via the mourners he has earlier mentioned, to his past in the theater. But it swings too far, for in the sentence about "the other room" and the "gods" who sit "Down there," Martin is glancing backward at his terror as a child of that presence lurking in the cellar, that force uncontrollable by his ego. In short, the sentence refers obliquely to his awarenesss of death, so he must yank himself back to the "faces" that are supposedly weeping for him alive. However, the thought that has intruded of death combines with Martin's physical awareness of the water (sweat) increasing around his ankles to drive his mind back—not so far, initially, as to his actual death in the sea—but to the escape from death that he created by "struggling, half-swimming, half-climbing" up the funnel of rock on the island. Having been pushed this far back towards its crucial experience, the ego gives way for a moment. Even in recollection, the escape fails: "The wall was turning over. . . ." And in the rest of the paragraph Martin again goes through his death by water ("that was burning him to the bone and past"), though the same sentences, on the simplest level, describe his envelopment in sweat.

But the ego is not yet defeated. With a thrust of energy, it reenacts its escape from death again:

He burst the surface and grabbed at a stone wall. There was hardly any light but he knew better than to waste time because of what was coming. There were projections in the wall of the tunnel so that though it was more nearly a well than a tunnel he could still climb. He laid hold, pulled himself up, projection after projection. The light was bright enough to show him the projections. They were faces, like the ones in the endless corridor. They were not weeping but they were trodden. They appeared to be made of some chalky material for when he put his weight on them they would break away so that only by constant movement upward was he able to keep up at all. He could hear his voice shouting in the well.

"I am! I am! I am!"

And all the time there was another voice that hung in his ears like the drooling of the Forces Programme. Nobody paid any attention to this voice but the nature of the cretin was to go on talking even though it said the same thing over and over again. . . .

"Tunnels and wells and drops of water all this is old stuff. You can't tell me. I know my stuff just sexual images from the unconscious, the libido, or is it the id? All explained and known. Just sexual stuff what can you expect? Sensation, all tunnels and wells and drops of water. All old stuff, you can't tell me. I know."

Intent upon avoiding the knowledge of "what was coming" (the black lightning that will wipe it out), the self again struggles up the tunnel of rock to escape the drowning, even though the tunnel becomes a vision of Martin's whole progress through life (which has been as dominated by his ego as is his drive to evade death). In spite of this vision, the ego proclaims its own identity—"I am! I am! I am!"—proclaims it even while fundamentally aware that the escape is an illusion, as is clear from the self's inability to make any headway up the tunnel and from its sense of inhabiting a place "more nearly a well than a tunnel." Desperately powerful as this assertion is, however, there remains something mechanical about the operation of the ego, suggested both by the image of Martin climbing and climbing to stay in the same spot and by the repetition of "I am." And this mechanical quality has its counterpart in the line taken by the rational mouth, out at the periphery of Martin's being: for the mouth, ironically enough, goes on manufacturing a

reasonable explanation in its talk about "sexual images."
But, for the moment, the mind and ego have won out, and
Martin has again postponed his admission of being dead.

Viewed as a whole, the passage is certainly an extreme
instance of the dense verbal texture in *Pincher Martin,* for
many of the images in the quoted paragraphs have values
which are multiple as well as constantly shifting. Yet the
passage is also essentially representative of the entire novel
in that, on any given page, Golding is likely to fuse several
apparently different levels of reality—memories of the past,
intimations of the actual death, the substantial world of the
rock, the ego's fight to survive—and to require that we separate them in order to interpret precisely the flow of Martin's
consciousness.

There is no question of a verbal surface complicated by
the representation of subjective processes in the closing chapter of *Pincher Martin,* which records the arrival of an officer
named Davidson at a remote island in the Hebrides to identify Martin's body, Davidson's conversations with Mr. Campbell—who has found the body—about death, and Davidson's
final assertion that Martin had no time to suffer because "He
didn't even . . . kick off his seaboots." But the chapter does
present a difficulty in interpretation. Many critics read it in a
strictly literal fashion and consider it a rather tricky and
inept device on Golding's part to reveal, at long last, Martin's death in the water.[6] It seems to me, however, that the
mode of the final chapter is essentially allegorical and that
the point of Golding's conclusion is to show how a human
type very different from Martin, Mr. Campbell, may behave
when facing death on a bare island.

Surely we are encouraged to think of Davidson not simply
as a naval officer but as Death itself. He comes on "a black

shape" out of the "west" and "a wintry sunset" (p. 202) ;
works "seven days a week" (p. 203) ; is repeatedly described
as a death's head, with "eyes that did not blink," eyes "just a
fraction too wide open" (p. 203), and "a grin without
humour" on the "lower part" of his face (p. 203). As for
Campbell, I would guess that his name is common enough,
especially in combination with the stripped-down locale, to
suggest that he is an Everyman. At least he is a more normal
sort than Martin: twice tipping his cap to Death humbly, in
contrast to Martin's arrogant rejection of death; continually
showing his compassion for others, whereas Martin is caught
up in himself; questioning, where Martin asserts; above all,
confronting Death and its mystery, whereas Martin has
sought to avoid them.

In the course of the final chapter, Campbell gradually
brings himself to meet the gaze of the officer and to study his
face, which is to say that he recognizes Davidson as Death.
And Davidson himself is represented with some consistency
as behaving in ways appropriate to that allegorical person-
age, it seems to me, in that Golding makes the officer regard
death primarily as a sheer recurrent fact rather than as an
event charged with the emotional and metaphysical complications that it has for Campbell. Thus Davidson's rather
superior air in dealing with Campbell; his interest in the
identity disk alone, as opposed to Campbell's human interest
in all the circumstances surrounding the discovered body (p.
204) ; and his dig at Campbell's lack of "second sight" (p.
206). All the unequivocal compassion in this meeting ema-
nates from Campbell, for the officer who must identify the
dead and for Martin himself.[7] Davidson's reactions and
words strike me as ambiguous. His drinking, before and
after identifying Martin's body, may be a mark of the stress
he feels as a man or a kind of toast to the newly dead. To

Campbell's expression of sympathy at the officer's daily task —"A sad harvest for you, Captain. I do not know how you can endure it"—Davidson replies, to the accompaniment of a disappearing "grin," "I wouldn't change [my job? my nature?]" (pp. 203–4) : a response which may mean either that, as a human, he is dutiful though distraught or that, as Death, he is devoted to his work. What Davidson says specifically about Martin, which might at first glance seem compassionate—"I have to thank you, Mr. Campbell, in the name of this poor officer" (p. 207), or his final assurance that Martin did not suffer—becomes grotesquely inappropriate if we remember the Martin we have seen throughout the novel. And, true to his role as Death, Davidson is simply "bewildered" when Campbell's questions become metaphysical.

Meanwhile, Campbell has progressed from admitting his own human fear of death (pp. 204–5) to watching, when Davidson goes to claim Martin in the hut, the very advent of death: he "contemplated the lean-to as though he were seeing it for the first time" and sees in its ruins "a profound and natural language that men were privileged to read only on a unique occasion" (p. 205). When Davidson returns from the hut, Campbell may flinch after having "read the face line by line as he had read the lean-to," but he goes on to look at Davidson "carefully, eye to eye"—and to raise the questions that every human would raise with Death, given the "chance" of a "meeting" like this, one "unpredictable and never to be repeated" (pp. 206–7). Studying the "wreck" of the lean-to again, which functions even more obviously now as a surrogate for the dead Martin, Campbell first asks what one is to make of life itself: "Would you believe that anything ever lived there?" Davidson is nonplused—"I simply don't follow you, I'm afraid" (p. 207) — so Campbell tries again, setting aside his "official beliefs" and extending his question to inquire about the possibility of life after death: "Would you say there was any—surviving? Or is that all? Like the lean-to?" But Davidson/Death evades this ultimate question, unable to answer it or unconcerned with it, and reverts instead to the physical facts of Martin's death, asserting that Campbell need not worry about the drowned man's suffering: "You saw the body. He didn't even have time to kick off his seaboots" (p. 208).

So Campbell is left at the close of the novel in the position of all of us. And in his role as Everyman through this final chapter, especially an Everyman who gets no answers to his questions about death, Campbell stands for the readers of the story, thus serving as a means—the naval officer in *Lord of the Flies* is another such, and Tuami in *The Inheritors* still another—by which Golding relates the preceding narrative and its issues more directly to his audience. But within the novel, as I have indicated, Golding uses Campbell's encounter with death to contrast in a variety of ways with Martin's. The underlying and vital difference between the two men is that Campbell accepts his limitations as a human being and as an individual. Golding dramatizes the fact most movingly, I think, in the last words Campbell utters in the novel: to Davidson's "If you're worried about Martin —whether he suffered or not—," Campbell replies, after a pause and a sigh, "Aye . . . I meant just that" (p. 208). For one thing, the response shows him admitting, as it were, that his previous metaphysical question about a life after death is not susceptible to a definitive answer in the human world; while his question has allowed for the sort of dimension to existence that Martin has been everywhere bent on denying, Campbell in effect acknowledges himself bound at last by the imperfection of human knowledge. His statement also betrays, in its concern with the suffering attendant on death, his own fears as an individual about that crisis, fears which—so his resignation suggests—he has settled himself to endure. But his reply also declares explicitly his compassion for Martin, that flow of feeling out from one ego to include another which is so notably lacking in Martin himself. In depicting Campbell as ordinary, as a person humanly limited who accepts his limitations, Golding provides an important counterpart to the central figure of the novel, who reveals his extraordinariness in his struggle—when faced with the proof of his limitations as man—to create out of his ego a universe that he would will to be self-sufficient and unbounded by death. But of course Martin fails; and, though his struggle may seem heroic at times, what the novel as a whole insists upon is that he is so compelled by the imperatives of the self, so utterly encased within himself, as to become monstrous.[8] Certainly his compulsion and the degree of his encasement are extreme, yet in a very general sense Martin may be said to take his place alongside the boys in *Lord of the Flies* and the new men in *The Inheritors* as a representative of the liabilities indigenous in the human condition. In *Free Fall,* Golding's fourth novel, he again treats a character terrifyingly imprisoned in self, but one who also has access to a different order of experience.

1. *"Pincher Martin,"* Radio Times, CXXXVIII, March 21, 1958, 8.

2. *The Two Deaths of Christopher Martin* (New York, 1957), pp. 76–77; this is the edition to which I give page references.

3. Critical opinion is divided on the question of whether the God who appears is real or an illusion of Martin's mind. It seems to me that he must be regarded as real, as a further intrusion of the non-egotistical on the world that Martin has imagined, if we take into account the

whole trajectory of the story; surely Martin's ego, acting in its own interest, would never dream up this manifestation of otherness. The problem of interpretation arises, I suppose, because Golding's fiction thus insists on the reality of God.

4. Golding himself has confirmed this interpretation in a private letter to John Peter: "The cellar in *Pincher Martin* represents more than childhood terrors; a whole philosophy in fact—suggesting that God is the thing we turn away from into life, and therefore we hate and fear him and make a darkness there" (quoted in *A Source Book,* p. 34).

5. Ironically enough, it would appear that Martin bears a heavy responsibility for the sinking of the destroyer, and so for his own death, because—in pursuing his plan to kill Nat—he has sent the port lookout below, the man who might have seen the torpedo approach. James Baker feels that the coinciding of the torpedo's explosion with Martin's order intended to dispose of Nat may suggest a moral judgment on Martin by some "agent or cosmic force" mysteriously at work in Golding's universe (*William Golding,* p. 46); I take the coincidence simply as commenting ironically on Martin in the ways that I have indicated. Frank Kermode has also written of these events, finding Martin's "order . . . freely willed and murderous," but "also necessary and proper in the circumstance" of the submarine's attack. If I am interpreting him properly, Kermode implies that Martin is aware of the approaching torpedo, but I miss the evidence for this in Golding's description of the incident. Kermode praises the multiple relevance of Martin's order—to avoiding the torpedo and to killing Nat—as an "invention" on the part of Golding that "Only the best in fiction" can offer (p. 117); to me, the coincidence seems too startling, too manufactured.

6. James Gindin objects to the ending because he feels that it reduces "the whole drama on the rock" to "a momentary flash in Martin's mind," and that this compression of time, in turn, undermines the story by finally compelling us to regard all that Martin has gone through as tinged with "parody" (*A Source Book,* p. 137). But for one thing, this objection presumes that most of the book transpires in an instant while Martin drowns, whereas the fiction of the novel seems to be that the ego continues to create a world for itself after the body has died. Secondly, Gindin understands the "drama on the rock" as a defeat by nature's forces of Martin's "sanity" and of "man's careful and calculated attempts to achieve salvation" (p. 137); but Martin's struggle in fact dramatizes how egocentric he is and how utterly he resists salvation. To such a struggle, an implication of parody—if it exists—might not

be inappropriate. Finally, I think Gindin misses the contrast with Martin's reaction to death provided by Mr. Campbell's reaction in the closing chapter, a subject I take up in my text.

7. One might interpret the sentence that follows, in which Campbell looks at the officer, as a possible exception to my claim about Davidson's lack of compassion: "He glanced up at the too-wide eyes, the face that seemed to know more than it could bear" (p. 204). But the statement may record Campbell's reading of the face, and in any case "seemed" is a qualified phrasing.

8. James Baker makes the same point in arguing against the claim that Martin is heroic: "Instead of depicting the assault of reality on the hapless soul of rational man, Golding shows the outrageous attack of a rational man, who is far more sick than heroic, upon nature and God" (*William Golding*, p. 40). Most often in his book, Baker views man's rationality as the enemy that Golding takes under attack, and *Pincher Martin* seems to me to provide the surest support for this thesis among Golding's novels—though even in this story, we may remember, the ego itself, not rationality, is the "dark centre." Later on in his discussion of *Pincher Martin,* Baker also seeks to check those who would read Golding in too determinedly Christian a fashion; but, though I sympathize with his intent, I think he goes too far in saying, "there is no risk in asserting that Golding's beleaguered castaways suffer and die in a universe which is more pagan than Christian" (p. 45). For it seems to me that a Christian orientation is always there in the novels, sometimes heavily muted, sometimes dominant. In the case of *Pincher Martin,* the narrative's focus on death, the presentation of God, and the thesis concerning the arrogance and limitations of man— so central a feature of Christianity, as well as of other systems of belief —all force the reader, I think, to imagine the story as unfolding in a Christian context.

IV

Free Fall

In one respect, *Free Fall* (1959) seems a clear corollary to its predecessor, *Pincher Martin.* Whereas Martin's ego compels him to deny the otherness of the universe and to regard the manifestation of God as a projection of the self, Sammy Mountjoy—at the moment of being sunk most completely in his self—can cry out for help, thereby acknowledging the otherness of the universe and indeed experiencing its divinity. This is not to say that *Free Fall* offers us a character who succeeds in transcending himself in any sustained fashion: its central figure remains as essentially limited by his humanity as someone like *Pincher Martin*'s Mr. Campbell. The defining condition of Sammy's existence—in fact, the point that William Golding is making in *Free Fall,* as I read the book —is the riddle of his awareness: for he both feels enclosed within a guilty self yet is periodically visited, when the demands of the self are in abeyance, by perceptions of the world about him as miraculous.

While the view of the human condition in *Free Fall* thus resembles in certain ways the view of man dramatized in *Pincher Martin,* many of Golding's methods in his fourth novel differ markedly from those employed in his earlier work. Instead of presenting the story from a technically omniscient vantage point, he casts *Free Fall* in the form of a first-person narrative, with Sammy Mountjoy, a famous painter, rehearsing and reflecting on his past. As a result of the shift to Sammy's perspective, the novel often moves at a leisurely pace, contains a number of intensely subjective, almost lyrical evocations by Sammy of his youth, and includes—because he is meditating on his past—a good deal of commentary. In *Free Fall,* Golding also provides us with a more detailed and ordinary social context than he has previously, placing Sammy's life against the background of twentieth-century England and isolating him only briefly in the sort of extraordinary situation that we have encountered in the first three books. Perhaps Golding's chief innovation in this novel, however, is his abandoning of the fundamentally linear plot typical of the earlier stories—where the relentless progress of events generated an ever-increasing narrative excitement—for an apparently disordered structure in which chronology is freely violated and events seem to occur when they do largely because Sammy has been somehow moved to recollect them.

Such departures have contributed to the sense shared by several of Golding's critics that *Free Fall* is different in its fictional mode from his previous books: that it is not a successful fable, though it may aspire to be one, but an essentially realistic novel that may or may not escape the liabilities of the genre. Frank Kermode names "the Fall of Man" as the book's subject, but feels that Golding has not sufficiently dramatized the myth through Sammy's experience, that too much of the story gives us "continuous comment . . . on the myth" rather than convincing reenactment of it (*A Source Book,* pp. 118–19). James Baker suggests that Golding achieves a kind of ultimate realism. Arguing that what Sammy finally discovers is the sheer "patternlessness" of his life, Baker continues: "There is no 'fable,' properly speaking, no symbolic artifice to accept or reject. *Free Fall* stands on the border between art and life. By taking up this extreme and tenuous position, it communicates" a "mystery and terror" transcending "all fable" (*William Golding,* p. 58). Samuel Hynes, like Kermode, thinks Sammy Mountjoy's commentary excessive, and he also finds the action of the novel uninformed by a controlling myth, so "the scenes . . . must be read, and must find their connections, on the literal level of action"; but even on this level, for Hynes, the scenes do not cohere and make up a significant structure

(*William Golding,* pp. 39–40). While some have claimed that Golding's first stories are threatened as convincing fictional structures because he so carefully adjusts all the details of the novelistic world to a paradigm of meaning, in *Free Fall* he would seem to be running an opposite risk: of including materials that do not eventuate in a realized paradigm of meaning.

Such problematic matters as the novel's organization, theme, and mode I shall be elaborating on in the course of this chapter. But a preliminary glance at the pages in which Sammy introduces his own story will indicate some of the difficulties that it raises. The narrative, he tells us, is to be built largely out of his recollections and will be ordered rather subjectively than chronologically, for the mode of time that is "memory," as he describes it, far from progressing steadily, involves "a sense of shuffle fold and coil, of that day nearer than that because more important, of that event mirroring this, or those three set apart, exceptional and out of the straight line altogether."[1] What in general impels Sammy to review his past is the drive to "understand" himself, but the "understanding" that he refers to in parts of this prologue seems to imply something other than a strictly rational grasp. For he insists on the limitations of "all systems" (pp. 6–7), though acknowledging his desire to find "a pattern that fits over everything I know" (p. 6); he recognizes man's inherent liability "to confuse" his own ideas "with the bounds of possibility and clap the universe into a rationalist hat or some other" (p. 9); and he proposes finally that in searching through his past he may discover, not "complete coherence," but "the indications of a pattern that will include me, even if the outer edges tail off into ignorance" (p. 9). The statements suggest that, at least from Sammy's point of view, his journey may result rather in a realization of his experience than in some controlling explanation of and accounting for it. His specific quest, he informs us, is for the moment when he lost his freedom, and again he distinguishes between one sort of knowledge that can be reasoned about, systematized, and another that is simply proved upon our pulses: "Free-will cannot be debated but only experienced" (p. 5). For Sammy, free will is a fact of his existence, as is the religious awareness to which he attests in the book's opening paragraph: ". . . I have felt the flake of fire fall, miraculous and pentecostal" (p. 5). And such existential facts, it seems to me, may have their own influence on the mode of the novel in that they would appear less susceptible to being dramatically exposited and developed than to being declared, merely presented as absolutes. They perhaps help to explain—along with Sammy's attempt to realize his past—why *Free Fall* strikes one as more assertive than fully dramatic in the manner of the earlier books, and why this novel seems in some ways static: aimed at defining the condition of a man rather than moving toward some clear-cut narrative and thematic resolution of his state. A last point about Sammy's prologue should be made. As a reason for writing his story, he cites the human compulsion to communicate, and then goes on to describe the impossibility of re-creating exactly one's inner being in words (p. 8). It would follow, then, that his first-person narrative is in itself an expression of Sammy's limitations as a human being, a reflection in the novel's form of the thesis about man that Golding pursues throughout *Free Fall*.

Some of these general points I have been making about *Free Fall* would suggest that Golding's undertaking here is in certain respects comparable to Conrad's in "Heart of Darkness." Both stories are essentially first-person narratives (though I do not mean to minimize the use that Conrad makes of the enclosing frame provided for his novella by Marlow's listeners) —narratives which the tellers feel compelled to relate. Both narrators are groping through their pasts and recalling events whose significance, though portentous, often seems beyond decisive formulation by the tellers. And despite the frequency with which they comment, both narrators are, I think, involved in that order of subjective experience which lends itself more readily to being lived through than to being analyzed and rationally comprehended by them. But a major difference between the stories would be this. In "Heart of Darkness" Conrad sketches for the reader, however obliquely, a precise moral development in Marlow, even though the narrator neither articulates the stages clearly as he goes through them nor arrives finally at an inclusive evaluation of what has happened to him as a person: in short, Conrad so manages his tale that the reader understands more, or at least more clearly, than Marlow. By the end of *Free Fall*, however, I believe that the reader remains, and is intended to remain, as limited in his knowledge as the narrator is—though several of Golding's critics have proposed that the reverse is true in an argument that I shall try to answer at the close of this chapter, when discussing the puzzling conclusion to *Free Fall* and the novel's meaning.

But first I must map out the controlling structure of the story and illustrate the principles according to which Golding organizes local segments of the narrative. Subsequently, I shall treat what seem to me certain weaknesses in Golding's characterization as well as in his conduct of the narrative. And then, before turning to the novel's conclusion and thesis, I want to draw attention to the style in which parts of

Free Fall are written, for at moments here Golding's prose differs radically from what we have seen in the earlier books.

In spite of Sammy's claims in the introductory pages about the waywardly subjective ordering of the story to follow and about not aspiring to "complete coherence," *Free Fall* in fact reveals itself as a structured whole. For, of course, no matter what Sammy himself may say, it is Golding who creates the novel, shaping the narrative and experience of his character into meaningful contours for the reader.[2] Even chronology is not so freely violated as Sammy's talk about the eccentric movements of memory might indicate. Roughly speaking, the first section of the story proper (Chapters 1–3) records Sammy's childhood; the second section (Chapters 4–6) skips over his adolescent years to detail his courting and sexual conquest, as a young art student, of Beatrice, the girl he desires so passionately; the third section (Chapters 7–10) leaps ahead to present Sammy as a man, a prisoner in a German concentration camp who is first interrogated by Dr. Halde, then shut up in solitary confinement, and at last released into a world which he sees as instinct with divinity; the fourth section (Chapters 11–12) shifts back radically in time to Sammy as a schoolboy, describing two teachers who affect him deeply, his first view of Beatrice and attempt to sketch her, then his conscious commitment to pursuing her; but the final section (Chapters 13–14) returns for the most part to Sammy's post-war present, showing his visit to Beatrice (now an idiot in an institution, perhaps as a result of Sammy's behavior) and his last fruitless efforts to communicate with the two teachers, his "spiritual parents"—though the closing page of the novel veers back in time to the moment of Sammy's release from solitary confinement in the prison camp.

In addition to this loosely chronological development, Golding employs another perfectly conventional structuring device in referring again and again to Sammy's search, announced in the prologue, for the point at which he lost his freedom: as Sammy reviews one block of his past after another, he asks whether the point is "Here," and his answer is always "Not here" until the end of the book's fourth section (the only one which is as a whole chronologically displaced in the narrative), where the adolescent Sammy has just determined to go after Beatrice at whatever cost. But I do not mean to suggest that the structure of *Free Fall* makes no demands upon the reader. Although the sequence of large blocks into which the story falls exhibits a reasonably clear dramatic and thematic logic, many of the most significant connections within a given section or between one section and another arise from such relatively oblique organizing forces as reiterated motifs, juxtapositions, and emerging parallels. Thus I shall work through the separate sections of the book once more to indicate the function of each in the logic of the whole and the ways in which the individual units are shaped, then turn to some of the parallels that act themselves to bind the separate units together and define Sammy's experience for us.

The chief function of the chapters in which Sammy recalls his childhood is to present him, prior to his loss of freedom, in his original guiltlessness. For all the squalor of his life with Ma in Rotten Row, he feels warmly related to, included in, the world about him. And the terrors, the adventures, even the cruelties and blasphemy of his early years turn out to be demonstrations of his innocence. One night he awakes in terror, sure that the clock by the bed has stopped ticking, so goes to fetch Ma from the pub, but they return to find that the clock has been ticking all the time and that it is the heart of their lodger in the room above which has stopped beating, the episode implying the special openness of the child to a transnatural order of experience. Similarly, when he invades a private estate with an equally guiltless friend, Johnny Spragg (in a kind of counterpart to their lawless invasion of an airfield, earlier in Chapter 2, which has resulted in an encounter with death when a pilot crashes), Sammy recalls that "we took nothing, almost we touched nothing. We were eyes" (p. 45), and his dominant impression is of a growing tree, miraculous in its beauty, which "Later, I should have called . . . a cedar and passed on, but then, it was an apocalypse" (p. 46). Even his escapades with the selfish Philip Arnold—who was "never a child" and constantly manipulated others because "He knew about people" (p. 49)—do not mar Sammy's fundamental innocence. He may be induced to bully the other kids for their fagcards and to defile the altar in the church (because Philip must test the curate's statement that God inhabits the altar), but these events do not mark Sammy spiritually because he is rather acting under Philip's influence than exercising his personal freedom to choose deliberately. At some moments through this first section Sammy shows signs of beginning to contract into a separate self: in the incident where the idiot schoolgirl Minnie wets on the floor when she cannot speak her name, Sammy delightedly decides, along with the other children, that "she was not one of us. . . . She was an animal down there, and we were all up here" (p. 35). But at the close of the section, after he has described his questioning by Father Watts-Watt, the rector of the church whose altar Sammy has violated, and a subsequent stay in the hospital (because a blow he received in the church has brought to a head a mastoid infection), Sammy can still imagine his childish self as lighted by "one of the colours" of heaven's "pure

white light" and judge the child "innocent of guilt, unconscious of innocence; happy, therefore, and unconscious of
happiness" (pp. 77–78).

The second unit of the novel contrasts sharply with the
first in representing a nineteen-year-old Sammy who has
already lost his freedom. Previously "unconscious of [his]
innocence," he now becomes increasingly aware of the degree to which he is trapped within himself through desiring
Beatrice, and the unit focuses on the curve of their relationship. Even the occasional glimpses that we catch of Sammy as
a member of the Young Communist League during this
period show him dominated by his local feelings for Beatrice, not by political conviction. (The particular group to
which he belongs devotes itself rather to the practice of
"freedom" in sexual matters than to Marxist politics, and
the only working class member has joined in hopes of advancing himself socially.) What draws Sammy to Beatrice,
aside from her physical attractiveness, is the compulsion he
feels to plumb the depths of her being—"I want to be you"
(p. 105)—in order to obliterate her separateness as a self
and to solve her "mystery" as a person. But his pursuit of her
turns more and more determinedly sexual, an act of aggres-
sion by the self. Thus his shame, on his first attempt to take
her, is so great that even his body cannot co-operate, and
after that he is driven to exploit her sexually with constantly
increasing violence in hope of achieving some sort of union
—while Beatrice, resigning herself to all that happens, can
respond only by becoming utterly dependent on him and
thus remains as fundamentally separate as ever. Their situation is imaged in Sammy's account (pp. 123–24) of a paint-
ing that he has made of Beatrice during this desperate time.
He has delineated her body, and in his "self-contempt" at
physically exploiting her he has "added the electric light-

shades of Guernica to catch the terror, but there was no terror to catch." The picture in fact shows a "light from the window" scattering "gold . . . over her breasts, her belly and her thighs"; and Sammy remembers that in her "face," which he could not paint, "There was dog faith and . . . submission," that "after my act and my self-contempt she lay, looking out the window as though she had been blessed." His description here also indicates what the whole assault on Beatrice has forced him to ignore: mired in his self, he cannot take account of the divine uniqueness inherent in her, as in any individual, nor can he accept the essential separateness of selves that is a limiting feature of the human condition. His relation to Beatrice having thus degenerated, Sammy suddenly meets Taffy, the daughter of a convert to Communism; they fall in love immediately and soon marry (despite the theories prevailing in the Young Communist League regarding sex) , with Sammy simply abandoning Beatrice and his earlier promise to marry her.

Whereas the second unit depicts a Sammy aware of having lost his freedom, the third dramatizes his fullest experience of imprisonment within his guilty self as he descends, in growing isolation, to the very limits of his being and is then accorded a vision of the universe as miraculous. The controlling narrative of these chapters is developed to some extent in the manner of Golding's earlier novels, moving irreversibly through a series of carefully graded steps to a shattering climax. Now a prisoner of war, Sammy is questioned by Dr. Halde about the escape of two captives from the German concentration camp, and the Doctor skillfully employs one device after another to break Sammy down: a friendly manner, sheerly rational appeals, a devastating analysis of Sammy's nature, temptations to every pleasure, a relativistic morality, and the threat of torture. Only towards the end of the interrogation does Sammy reveal to us that he may indeed have some information, but he still resists disclosing it, so is shut up in what seems to him a dark cell. After an intervening chapter in which he thinks back to his early life in the home of Father Watts-Watt (who has adopted Sammy on the boy's release from the hospital) and describes his "generalized," innocent fear of the dark as a child, Sammy goes on to portray his local terror at the blackness of the cell, a terror that turns out to be engendered by his guilt, for it finally becomes clear that the decisive cell confining Sammy is his own self. In the course of the chapter, he explores the sides and center of the physical cell with excruciating slowness in an effort to discover what horrors Dr. Halde may have devised (at the center he finds what he takes—according to Mark Kinkead-Weekes and Ian Gregor, *William Golding,* p. 184—to be a penis, a token of what his mature existence amounts to). But Sammy also keeps implying that all the imagined horrors may be the work of his own mind, as indeed they prove, rather than of the ingenious Dr. Halde. Nevertheless, as the pressure of his isolation mounts, Sammy is transformed from a frightened prisoner hoping to retain whatever information he may possess into a more and more irrational being who is at last reduced to the level of an animal crying out instinctively for help.

The paragraphs that conclude the chapter (on pp. 184–85) render a moment of experience that Sammy himself believes central to his life, and the sustained ambiguity that I sense in them appears to me crucial to our understanding of the novel. His first "Help me! Help me!" is "the cry of the rat when the terrier shakes it," sheerly "instinctive," undirected at anyone on earth or in heaven, uttered "not with hope of an ear but as accepting a shut door, darkness and a shut sky." Yet as Sammy says, "the very act of crying out changed the thing that cried," and he begins to cast about for some source of aid, looking "with starting and not physical eyes on every place, against every wall, in every corner of the interior world." Although he calls out "Help me!" once more, his searches reveal only the "absolute" of his own "helplessness" and the impossibility of any evasion in his present situation. Since there is apparently no escape either from the blighted self or the physical cell, continues Sammy, "the snake, the rat struck again from the place away from now into time. . . . struck at the future":

> The future was the flight of steps from terror to terror, a mounting experiment that ignorance of what might be a bribe, made inevitable. The thing that cried fled forward over those steps because there was no other way to go, was shot forward screaming as into a furnace, as over unimaginable steps that were all that might be borne, were more. . . . The thing that screamed left all living behind and came to the entry where death is close as darkness against eyeballs.
> And burst that door.

The primary narrative sense of all these paragraphs in the context of the whole chapter is that Sammy has reached the end of his resistance and seeks release from the cell to confess what he knows about his fellow prisoners, however unsure he is concerning what Dr. Halde may still have in store for him and however tortured he feels at the prospect of betraying his comrades. But simultaneously the paragraphs display Sammy arriving at the boundaries of the self and recognizing his limitations as a guilty human in his call for help. The change in "the thing that cried" which has been produced by "the very act of crying" would indicate an incipient acknowledgment on Sammy's part of some power that transcends the self to which he has been enslaved. And the agonizing "future" that he represents may be read as the tortured existence Sammy imagines for a self which remains conscious of its own guilt while it sees the surrounding universe as charged with divinity. Golding manages the passage, I am arguing, in such a way that Sammy's most extreme confinement within himself—expressed in his readiness to betray his companions—coincides with his breakthrough to a transcendent vision. In effect, the paragraphs dramatize a miracle.[3]

The closing chapter of the third section presents Sammy at large in the prison camp, looking at the world about him, himself, and his past through "dead eyes"—"dead" both because, I think, he has undergone a kind of moral death through his willingness to betray his companions and certainly because for the moment he has transcended his ordinary nature to the degree of seeing selflessly. The earth and mankind stand forth for him in all their miraculousness. "Everything is related to everything else," he finds, in a universe that is saturated with "love" and even contains a heaven, though that "place" is "sometimes open and sometimes shut" for man, "the business of the universe proceeding there in its own mode, different, indescribable" (pp. 186–87). When Sammy turns his eyes on his self, the entity he perceives is as vile as Dr. Halde has claimed, but also "miraculous" in its creativity:

> . . . it continually defied the law of conservation of energy . . . and created shapes that fled away outwards along the radii of a globe. These shapes could be likened to nothing but the most loathsome substances that man knows of, or perhaps the most loathsome and abject crea-

tures, continuously created, radiating swiftly out and disappearing from my sight; and this was the human nature I found inhabiting the centre of my own awareness. (p. 190)

Even the Beatrice who has been earlier regarded by Sammy as so empty a figure can now be remembered as a "full" personality. Indeed, as a result of his revelation in the prison yard, Sammy is forever marked, "visited by a flake of fire, miraculous and pentecostal" (p. 188). The novel's third section as a whole may prove how truly Dr. Halde diagnoses Sammy's secular self while interrogating him:

> "There is no health in you, Mr. Mountjoy. You do not believe in anything enough to suffer for it or be glad. . . . You possess yourself. . . . Only the things you cannot avoid, the sear of sex or pain, avoidance of the one suffering repetition and prolongation of the other, this constitutes what your daily consciousness would not admit, but experiences as life." (pp. 144–45)

But the Doctor also acknowledges a "mystery" in his prisoner "which is opaque to both of us" (p. 145), thus requiring that Sammy be confined until he breaks, and the end of the third section reveals how unpredictably this "mystery" has developed into Sammy's experience of the divine.

The fourth block of *Free Fall* swings back in time to review Sammy's adolescent years and finally pinpoint the moment at which he lost his freedom. As Mark Kinkead-Weekes and Ian Gregor have maintained, the logic binding this to the previous section is one involving the insight of Sammy himself: he can isolate his original fall only after he has come to know, through his experience in the prison camp, the depth to which he has fallen (*William Golding,* p. 187). These chapters describing Sammy as a schoolboy are shot through with intimations of the children's growing self-consciousness, particularly with regard to sex. They also provide us with detailed portraits of the two teachers who have influenced Sammy so powerfully that he calls them his "spiritual parents." Fastidious Miss Pringle has the gift of making the Biblical miracles come alive for him, though she seems often to prefer explaining them rationally to her class. But she hates Sammy, and, when he mentions the "backparts" of the Lord, she mercilessly humiliates him in front of the class, violates his private notebook to construe his sketch of a landscape as an obscene picture of the human body, then isolates him in a corner of the schoolroom for the remainder of the term. Selfless Nick Shales is a thoroughgoing rationalist who denies "the spirit behind creation" (p. 214) to describe the universe entirely in terms of scientific laws, yet so impressive are his explanations that what he conveys to Sammy is a vision of an extraordinarily lovely cosmic dance.[4] Although the "world of miracle" associated with Miss Pringle is Sammy's natural habitat, he chooses the scientific universe of Nick Shales because of the man's personal kindliness—and then himself develops Nick's rationalism into a relativistic morality that will justify his pushing after Beatrice. She is a classmate whom he has noticed clearly only after sketching her one day for Philip Arnold, but her attraction constantly increases until, by the end of the fourth section, he knowingly surrenders himself to his desire for her. Out walking in the woods, and still sensing the divinity of the world though also seeing the fecundity of nature as a counterpart to his own sexual excitement, Sammy comes to a stream in which he is invited to bathe by "the angel of the gate of paradise," who would thus insure that Sammy's choice be uninfluenced by the tempting "spices of the forest" (p. 236). But Sammy's immersion in the water turns out to be a baptism in reverse, for he steps forth from the stream to experience to the full his physical self, to recognize precisely what he is and what he is bent upon, to taste his freedom once more, and then to lose it in dedicating himself—willing to sacrifice "Everything" (p. 236)—to the pursuit of Beatrice.

The purpose of the final unit in *Free Fall* is to bring us up towards the present time in which Sammy narrates his story and to insist, as I understand the book, that his predicament as a limited human being remains unresolved. He goes to see Beatrice in an asylum (who responds to his visit by wetting on the floor as the idiot child Minnie did years earlier), and Sammy acknowledges his guilt in behaving towards her as he has even while he recognizes that he may not be solely responsible for what she has become. He accepts the reproaches of Dr. Enticott on disclosing his earlier history with Beatrice although they are only about half-deserved, for the doctor is in part so angry because he himself has fallen in love with Sammy's wife. When Sammy seeks out Nick Shales to pay tribute to the man's innocence and to suggest that Nick has chosen rationalism irrationally, he finds his old teacher dying and cannot say what is in his mind, overwhelmed by a sense of "my own nothingness" (p. 251). It proves just as impossible for him to communicate with Miss Pringle, whom he hopes to forgive for her cruelty, but who now receives him as a favored pupil. As the novel moves to its close, Sammy contemplates first his vision of a scientifically explicable universe and then his vision of a moral universe informed by "the spirit," declaring that "both worlds are real. There is no bridge" before his mind swings back at last to his release from the cell—which turns out to have been a "cupboard" for "buckets" and "floorcloths"— and to the obscure words of the commandant who freed him: "The Herr Doctor does not know about peoples" (p. 253).

By rehearsing *Free Fall* in such detail, I have hoped not only to point up the dramatic logic of the story's units as a sequence but to make clear how recurrently Golding underscores his theme through representing Sammy as at once conscious of the miraculous and locked within his secular self. Other bearings that define Sammy's condition for us are provided by the many parallels which crop up between the separate sections and thus also serve to bind his recollections into a significant whole. Two of the more obvious parallels I have already touched on. The repetition by Beatrice in the asylum of Minnie's act in the schoolroom affects the reader as a measurement of Sammy's guilt in exploiting Beatrice so ruthlessly. In the same way, Golding uses two pictures of Beatrice done by Sammy to distinguish sharply between the states of innocence and guilt in the chief character. The earlier drawing (though Sammy does not describe it for us until the fourth section of *Free Fall*) is dashed off at the request of Philip Arnold before Beatrice has emerged as a person for Sammy. Since the demands of his self have not yet materialized, Sammy can capture her face and figure on paper as he never will again, the very strokes of his pencil mirroring his transcendent state:

The line leapt, it was joyous, free, authoritative. It achieved little miracles of implication so that the viewer's eye created her small hands. . . . That free line had raced past and created her face, had thinned and broken where no pencil could go, but only the imagination. (p. 221)

And when he looks at the model herself, he sees Beatrice for the moment in all her divine uniqueness, her countenance irradiated by the "light of heaven": ". . . I saw there in her face and around the openness of her brow, a metaphorical light that none the less seemed to me to be an objective phenomenon, a real thing" (p. 222). The later picture (which I have referred to in discussing the second section of *Free Fall*) marks how far Sammy has sunk within himself. He can paint only her body, reproducing "the finished perfection of her sweet, cleft flesh" (p. 123). But the essential Beatrice escapes him. For "the electric light-shades" that he has added "to catch the terror" prove "an irrelevance" since "there was no terror to catch," even the body of Beatrice in the picture remaining illuminated by a "gold" light from the window. And the face of the model, as the adult Sammy can recall, reveals a Beatrice who appears to him miraculously "blessed" in spite of what he has done to her (p. 124).

The last features of *Free Fall*'s structure that I shall glance at are two sets of parallels which operate less obviously yet more extensively than those just noted. We might more properly regard them, indeed, as limited segments of two recurring motifs, for instances of undergoing interrogation and torturing others abound in the story, but to chart those motifs fully would require too much space. The first parallel, which develops inversely in part, juxtaposes Sammy's defiling of the altar and subsequent questioning by the church authorities when a boy with his interrogation as a man by Dr. Halde and consequent revelation. The young Sammy is innocent, the mere tool of his friend, and when he tries to spit on the altar, the revelation that ensues is parodic: "The universe exploded" into pain at the blow of the verger who suddenly materializes in the darkness (p. 61), and, far from being God-like, he exhibits himself as an uncomprehending adult who imagines Sammy to be the agent of an organized conspiracy against the church. As questioners, the verger and Father Watts-Watt behave with none of Dr. Halde's menace (indeed, later demonstrate their compassion for the boy), but they direct their questions towards the disclosure of a plot about which Sammy knows nothing, and they ask them without any awareness of what a child is like, so get nowhere with Sammy. The session ends when he is "saved" by fainting away, overcome by the sheerly physical effects of the blow on his ear (p. 66). In the concentration camp, however, the adult Sammy is a guilty being, one who has sought consciously to violate Beatrice and who in fact possesses the kind of information that Dr. Halde is after. The Doctor's initial "friendliness" may be as "genuine" as Sammy thinks it (p. 134), but he conducts the questioning with merciless efficiency, and he knows as much about Sammy's nature as a man can. Although Sammy faints during the interrogation, he comes to again, and the disintegration that he ultimately undergoes in the cell is of his rational and moral rather than of his physical self, with the breakdown brought on less through Dr. Halde than through the workings of Sammy's own guilt. By the close of the whole episode, he is ready to tell what he knows, but he is miraculously saved and experiences in a state of transcendent consciousness a revelation of the universe as divine.

As I have already suggested, *Free Fall* contains more passages involving interrogation than those I have just described, notably one in which Miss Pringle questions Sammy relentlessly about his reading of the Bible and his exercise book. Similarly, the novel includes a number of sequences that show one character in effect torturing another, an example being Miss Pringle's pitiless treatment of Sammy. But the particular parallel that I shall take up here allies Sammy's behavior towards Beatrice with Dr. Halde's towards Sammy. Initially sympathetic to Beatrice, Sammy is caught in the machine of his sexual desire and thrusts on to plumb her "mystery" as a person, justifying his assault rationally on the ground that "Life . . . was relative" (p. 108). He subjects her to more and more pressure, threatening once to "kill" her (p. 106), but the ironic result of Sammy's exploitation is that he becomes blind to the individuality of Beatrice, that manifestation of the divine in her, and can only regard her as a secular object. Dr. Halde, too, evidences some sympathy for Sammy at first, but he has lost his freedom in becoming part of a "social machine" (p. 140) and is thus compelled to probe the "mystery" in Sammy by every available means (p. 145). He tempts Sammy with various bribes; tries to persuade him rationally through a relativistic argument that runs, "Which of us is right? . . . The problem is insoluble . . . [given] our sense of truth being nothing but an infinite regression, a shifting island in the middle of chaos—" (p. 151); and threatens finally to "kill" him (p. 152). When Dr. Halde arranges for his prisoner to be shut up in the darkness, he presumably foresees that Sammy will descend farther into his secular self, though the ironic result is Sammy's eventual release into a new consciousness of the divine. This set of parallels insists, of course, that Sammy has proceeded as ruthlessly with Beatrice as Dr. Halde does with him. And the whole novel reverberates with echoes like these which connect one of Sammy's memories with another and so inform his narrative with a firmer shape than appears on one's first reading of *Free Fall*.

Through defending the novel's structure as I have, I do not mean to imply that *Free Fall* is without weaknesses. Two

of them seem to me discernible in or related to the narrative
form, while two more seem matters of characterization, one
of them a case in which the paleness of the figure is attribut-
able to Golding's theme and the other a case in which the
function of the character is obscure. At least for me, the
narrative sags in the chapter describing Sammy's early days
in the house of Father Watts-Watt and his innocent fear of
the dark, a chapter placed between the interrogation by Dr.
Halde and Sammy's solitary confinement in the prison camp.
To be sure, this shift back into the past juxtaposes Sammy's
innocence to his adult guilt, providing us also with our most
detailed portrait of Father Watts-Watt, and the interruption
of the narrative creates suspense by holding us back from the
climax of Sammy's imprisonment. But the chapter is rather
too long for what it accomplishes and so slowly paced that it
retards drastically the controlling narrative thrust of the
third section towards the high point of Sammy's release.
Golding's narrative form generates another difficulty in the
second section of *Free Fall,* which sketches the curve of
Sammy's relation to Beatrice. The dramatic logic of the unit
requires Sammy to abandon Beatrice heartlessly as a demon
stration of his utter selfishness. But his separation from her
comes about at least in part because he meets Taffy, with
whom he engages in a relationship defined by their immediate and total commitment to each other. So the exhibition of
his selfishness with regard to Beatrice is to some degree
undermined by the quality of his experience with Taffy. And
I must add that this unique attachment binding Sammy with
Taffy is sketched by Golding in a rather perfunctory fashion,
an unfortunate consequence, perhaps, of the local narrative
demand that he weight Sammy's deserting of Beatrice.

The characterization of Beatrice herself strikes me as another shortcoming in *Free Fall.* We see her in the main—es-

pecially during those scenes of the second unit which establish her initially and give us our most sustained view of her —through the eyes of a fallen Sammy, and Golding's theme dictates that Sammy should become more and more blind to her. Thus to the reader, as to Sammy, she appears remote, contained, naïve, conventional, essentially empty as a person —and so fails to capture our sympathy as fully as she ought.[5] We may accept her physical attractiveness, but Sammy's blindness to her inner self prevents her from developing for us into a character rich enough to warrant the compulsion he feels to fuse his being with hers. And after we have been so long exposed to a relatively vacuous Beatrice, Sammy's discovery in the German camp that her "negative personality" was all the time "full" (p. 191) puts us under a strain, as does his later account of the young Beatrice instinct with divinity whom he saw on first drawing her. For we are so dominated by our impression in the earlier pages, where Golding represents Beatrice rather flatly because of his thesis concerning Sammy, that the later claims about her roundness as a character seem assertive and do not convince us dramatically.

Golding's handling of Dr. Enticott reveals a weakness of a different kind, I think. He is the man who has arranged Sammy's visit to Beatrice in the institution without knowing about their past and thus fears that his future as a doctor may be ruined; who savagely berates Sammy even though admitting to him that it is impossible to decide whether Sammy made Beatrice the idiot she is or saved her temporarily from becoming what she has; but who in part rails as he does because he loves Sammy's wife, wants to "share" in Sammy's existence with Taffy, and indeed declares, "In a sense I'm in love with both of you" (p. 249). Certainly the episode as a whole makes clear that Sammy's earlier actions have proliferating consequences which involve other persons, and Sammy himself acknowledges this to the full. But are we to view Dr. Enticott as a young Sammy caught within the self: worried about his professional career, cruelly abusive under pressure, tormented by an irreconcilable conflict between his love for Taffy, his jealousy of Sammy, and his desire to share in their life together? Or are we to see him as a foil to Sammy, a young man who will escape Sammy's predicament by renouncing his love for Taffy, for, when he asks what he should do, Sammy replies, "Look. You haven't hurt us. It will pass. Nothing of what you go through now will peer over your shoulder or kick you in the face" (p. 249) — predicting a future for Dr. Enticott unblighted by the sort of guilty consciousness that haunts the adult Sammy? As far as I can make out, the text lends itself to both interpretations, and the function of Dr. Enticott as a character remains obscure.

While *Free Fall* betrays certain weaknesses in Golding's management of narrative form and of his characters, the novel shows him at his most adventurous in the matter of style. I have already mentioned the looser rhythms in many segments of Sammy's first-person narrative and the lyric intensity of several moments when he recaptures his feelings as a child. But *Free Fall* departs most radically from the earlier books in requiring Golding to represent again and again the religious awareness of his chief character. Sometimes he defines Sammy's plight through an imagery that combines the religious with the secular, as in the passage leading up to Sammy's loss of freedom, a portion of which follows:

As for the heavy sky, the blue to purple, it filled every shape between the trees with inch-thick fragments of

stained glass, only at arm's length out of reach. The high
fronds touched my throat or caught me round the thighs.
There was a powder spilled out of all living things, a spice
which now made the air where I waded thick. In base-
ments of the forest among drifts of dried leaves and crack-
ling boughs, by boles cathedral thick, I said in the hot air
what was important to me; namely the white, unseen body
of Beatrice Ifor. . . . (p. 235)

Sometimes, as in the description of the universe that Sammy
sees on his release from the cell, Golding simply presents the
miraculous as literal fact, a sheer occurrence which, in all its
inexplicableness, remains one of the continuing givens of
Sammy's existence:

Huge tears were dropping from my face into dust; and
this dust was a universe of brilliant and fantastic crystals,
that miracles instantly supported in their being. I looked
up beyond the huts and the wire . . . accepting all things
and giving all created things away. . . . Those crowded
shapes extending up into the air and down into the rich
earth, those deeds of far space and deep earth were aflame
at the surface and daunting by right of their own natures
though a day before I should have disguised them as
trees. Beyond them the mountains were not only clear all
through like purple glass, but living. They sang and were
conjubilant. . . . The power of gravity, dimension and
space, the movement of the earth and sun and unseen
stars, these made what might be called music and I heard
it. (pp. 186–87)

And sometimes, as in the first paragraph of *Free Fall*,
Golding achieves a prose whose vocabulary, phrasing, and

rhythm work wonderfully together to create a religious aura and dramatize Sammy's condition as a limited human:

> I have walked by stalls in the market-place where books, dog-eared and faded from their purple, have burst with a white hosanna. I have seen people crowned with a double crown, holding in either hand the crook and flail, the power and the glory. I have understood how the scar becomes a star, I have felt the flake of fire fall, miraculous and pentecostal. My yesterdays walk with me. They keep step, they are grey faces that peer over my shoulder. I live on Paradise Hill, ten minutes from the station, thirty seconds from the shops and the local. Yet I am a burning amateur, torn by the irrational and incoherent, violently searching and self-condemned. (p. 5)

Obvious are the Biblical echoes both in diction—e.g., "purple," "hosanna," and "the crook and flail"—and in phrasing —"My yesterdays walk with me." But the rhythms, so patterned and so sustained, are what give the passage its firmest religious imprint, and they act out a drama of their own. The first three sentences testify to Sammy's view of life as miraculous, their unity underlined by the stately anaphora of "I have walked," "I have seen," "I have understood." The first sentence itself receives a rhythmic lift through the suspended unit in its middle, which makes the sentence erupt into a climax at its close. And, after the rhythm subsides a little in the second sentence, settling itself in the repeated doubling of the nouns, it quickens again in the third sentence—where the "miraculous" is specifically named for the first time—through the piling of one clause on top of the other (instead of a pairing by "and") . This third sentence is further colored, of course, by the marked alliteration; and one may even imagine that the idea of a miraculous transformation finds its verbal analogue in the conversion of a "scar" into a "star," where the change of one letter makes all the difference. The fourth sentence, appropriately brief, is the hinge of the paragraph, Sammy's attention now swinging toward the secular components of his past and present— though he does not reveal his own condition unequivocally until the final word of the paragraph. The fifth sentence, referring to the "grey faces" of the past that haunt Sammy, imitates in some degree the rhythm of the third, also splitting into two parallel clauses separated by a comma. And the sixth, with its series, is perhaps dimly reminiscent of the largest structural outlines of the second sentence. In part, the concluding sentence recapitulates the paragraph. It does so logically in Sammy's claim to be a "burning amateur"—a human being burned both by the pentecostal fire he has felt and by the hell of his secular self—as well as in his representation of himself as simultaneously "torn" by his inexplicable religious experience and yet committed to "violently searching" as mere man. Rhetorically, too, the sentence echoes what has gone before, to some extent, in its doubled terms and its alliteration. But this final sentence is also rhythmically climactic. For each of the previous sentences has closed with the same falling cadence (with the possible exception of the fourth, though I think the context makes one hear its cadence as rhythmically equivalent to the others) : "hosánna," "the glóry," "pentecóstal," "walk wíth me," "my shóulder," "the lócal." With "sélf-condémned," the closing cadence varies for the first time, the rhythmic shift emphasizing, most appropriately, the crucial fact about Sammy and his fall, a matter which the rest of the novel is devoted to exploring. In its significance, then, the paragraph turns out to be a microcosm of the whole story, showing

Sammy subject to the antagonistic forces which define the riddle of his existence as man. (Mark Kinkead Weekes and Ian Gregor have made the same point in their book, *William Golding*, p. 168.) As prose, the passage both initiates the record of his life that Sammy will set down and, through the style's evocation of the religious, begins to establish that other dimension of experience which comes to loom so large in the novel.

Throughout these pages discussing *Free Fall*, I have been hoping to indicate how frequently Golding represents Sammy's existence as a riddle, for this seems to me the governing thesis of the novel. The riddle is reflected in the book's title itself, which refers Sammy's fall both to the scientific universe of physics and to the theological world of the Bible. His last name, "Mountjoy," alludes primarily to Sammy's sexual activities, but it perhaps alludes as well to his capacity for briefly transcending his ordinary self to experience visions of the divine. Certainly the "Paradise Hill" where the guilty Sammy lives as an adult is also the place where, as an innocent child, he had his apocalyptic perception of a growing tree; moreover, the Hill is the location at once of the happy home which Sammy shares with Taffy and of the institution in which he knows the idiot Beatrice to dwell. And a host of other details in the story render comparable muddles. Just before Sammy dedicates himself to the pursuit of Beatrice, for instance, the headmaster of his school offers him some advice which is "true and powerful—therefore dangerous": "If you want something enough, you can always get it provided you are willing to make the appropriate sacrifice. . . . But what you get is never quite what you thought" (p. 235). The fallen Sammy, as we have already noted, can paint only the body of Beatrice, but what he later remembers is the "blessed" expression on her "hidden face" (p. 124). In the concentration camp, Sammy does indeed have some information to impart to Dr. Halde but does not know whether the information will prove sufficiently helpful. And according to the final verdict of Dr. Enticott, Sammy may or may not be responsible for the idiocy of Beatrice: there is no telling.

Nor does Sammy stand alone among the persons of *Free Fall* in exhibiting the muddle of man's condition. To be sure, several of the characters are reduced to single dimensions, thus serving in one way or another to emphasize some feature of Sammy's past: Ma is simply "there" (p. 16), a massive physical presence at the center of Sammy's earliest recollections; Johnny Spragg is thoroughly innocent and unselfconscious; Philip Arnold is as unrelievedly guilty and self-conscious. But most of the other figures reveal some fundamental contradiction. Dr. Halde is threatening yet friendly, satanic yet ascetic, committed to his rational analysis of Sammy's nature yet aware of some residual "mystery" in his prisoner. Father Watts-Watt is possessed by the fantasy of a plot against his church and himself, yet treats with real kindness the boy who has desecrated his altar—even though Father Watts-Watt is moved in part by his homosexual desire for Sammy, whom he takes into his own home, with perverse heroism, as a way of conquering the attraction he feels. Miss Pringle is the professed champion of the Bible, though given to explaining its miracles rationally, but she practises sadism in her dealings with all her pupils, torturing Sammy with a special ferocity because she thinks that he has usurped the place that belongs to her in the heart of Father Watts-Watt. Nick Shales, the convinced rationalist who denies the presence of "spirit" in the "cosmos," is nevertheless saintly, selfless, filled with "a love of people" (p. 213); and his choice itself of rationalism has been illogical, as Sammy tells us, a reaction against the cruel God of Power exalted in the Victorian days of Nick's youth. But of course Sammy himself remains the chief exemplar of man's muddle. His choice of Nick's universe, which initiates his own loss of freedom, is as illogical as Nick's, for to the adolescent Sammy,

> The beauty of Miss Pringle's cosmos was vitiated because she was a bitch. Nick's stunted universe was irradiated by his love of people. Sex thrust me strongly to choose and know. Yet I did not choose a materialistic belief. I chose Nick. For this reason truth seems unattainable. I know myself to be irrational because a rationalist belief dawned in me and I had no basis for it in logic or calm thought. (p. 226)

And the decisive vision through which the fallen Sammy regains a measure of freedom in the concentration camp, the "new mode of knowing" which he achieves when granted the power to see selflessly, is fraught with similar contradictions:

> At least I can tell when I acquired or was given the capacity to see. . . . In freedom I should never have acquired any capacity. Then was loss of freedom the price exacted, a necessary preliminary to a new mode of knowing? But the result of my helplessness out of which came the new mode was also the desperate misery of Beatrice and the good joys of Taffy. (p. 133)

The riddle of Sammy's nature has its counterpart in the ambiguities of the major events in *Free Fall*. His attempt to spit on the altar can be reckoned as innocent, despite his local feelings of guilt; the ensuing revelation is a parody of omnipotence, and the adults who would punish him turn instead into his protectors. The passage that renders Sammy's last moments in solitary confinement, as I have already argued, shows him approaching his most selfish act, the willing betrayal of his comrades, at the same time that he is being in part delivered from the self through recognizing its utter helplessness. The "scar" of Sammy's guilt is in the process of being miraculously transformed into the "star" that images the vision of the divine soon to be accorded him in the yard of the prison camp. No wonder the experience is crucial for him, yet it defines the riddle of his existence rather than solving it. Golding insists upon this fact, it seems to me, in the very last paragraphs of the novel (p. 253), where he describes the actual occasion of Sammy's release from confinement in such a way as to leave Sammy and the reader faced with the sorts of muddle that pervade the rest of *Free Fall*. When the door opens, Sammy walks out, expecting to meet "the judge," Dr. Halde, but it is the commandant of the prison camp who stands there and apologizes to Sammy for the confinement: "This should not be happening. I am sorry." Sammy looks back at the "cell" to discover that it is merely "an ordinary cupboard" for storing "buckets" and "floorcloths," which reveals that his tortures have been self-engendered in the main, though the possibility of Dr. Halde's devilish ingenuity remains, for Sammy refers to one cloth as "perhaps left . . . deliberately" behind, that piece of material which Sammy in his terror has imagined to be a male organ. In sending Sammy "back to the camp," the commandant utters the final words of the novel: "The Herr Doctor does not know about peoples." But is he declaring his compassion as a human for Sammy? Or is he speaking rather as a prison official who regrets and would dissociate himself from the methods employed by Dr. Halde, a member of the Gestapo (near the beginning of Sammy's interrogation, the deputy commandant has quarreled with Dr. Halde—when Sammy invokes the Geneva Convention—and been ordered to leave)? Or does the commandant merely testify to a stuffy Germanic propriety in apologizing for the confinement of his prisoner in so unsuitable a place? Surely the commandant's statement about the "Herr Doctor" is both untrue and true: Dr. Halde knows a tremendous amount about "peoples," especially Sammy, but he cannot foresee the spiritual illumination granted the fallen man. None of these ambiguities is resolved by Golding in the response of Sammy, for to him the words of the commandant are "inscrutable," "words that I should puzzle over as though they were the Sphinx's riddle," the tense of "should puzzle over" demonstrating that for Sammy the "riddle" will continue.

Many of the ambiguities just cited that inhere in the final paragraphs of *Free Fall* have also been spelled out by Mark Kinkead-Weekes and Ian Gregor, who interpret the evidence differently to offer a more optimistic reading of the novel's close (*William Golding*, pp. 194–99). They argue that Sammy is freed by a commandant who in part represents "Compassion"; that on the last page of the story "Golding himself takes over" and "moves beyond" Sammy; that the reader has come to sense more of Sammy's situation than does Sammy himself, and so may understand one of the commandant's lines (which the critics slightly misquote as "Have you heard?") to bear the meaning "Have you heard . . . that you are free, forgiven"; and that the book finally suggests to the reader, at least, how the divided world of Sammy may be integrated by the working of the divine:

Sammy's pattern of mutually exclusive modes would only have to be altered by bringing them, superimposed, into the same focus; but this is the whole difference between single and double vision. And there is no achievement of single vision: only a cryptic challenge to try it for ourselves in its astonishing difficulty. . . .

Attractive as such a reading is, however, I cannot feel that the novel sustains the distinctions which the critics propose, either between its author and Sammy—for there is no technical shift in perspective on the last page—or between Sammy's knowledge and the reader's. On Sammy's release into the yard of the prison, for instance, he is surely as conscious as a reader that his deliverance from the cell is undeserved and that the vision with which he finds himself rewarded is divinely begotten. And when, at the close of the book, the commandant in fact asks, "You have heard?" (a phrasing which to my ear a little resists translation into the direct question that the critics make of it), Sammy replies, "I heard"—which then would have to include the meaning, if the critics have interpreted the sense of the question correctly, that Sammy *has* heard of his being "free" and "forgiven," a meaning that would seem to conflict with their claim that "there is no achievement of single vision." I do not want to deny that Sammy *may* be "forgiven," but he has exactly the same grounds for believing it that we have, and for him the experience of the divine, the miraculous, remains but one component of his muddled being. Certainly he is not "free" by the conclusion of the story, still inhabiting the self whose irreconcilable contradictions may dissolve, according to ordinary Christian doctrine, only after death.

Through making so much of the many riddles in *Free Fall* and of its ambiguous close, I have been intending to stress Golding's absolute honesty in developing the thesis of the novel. For, although he endows his leading character with the capacity for religious experience, Golding does not thereby solve Sammy's problem as a human, refusing to present Sammy's visions and insights as reconciling a divided consciousness. The bonds of the self may slacken from time to time. As an artist, Sammy has known moments of being possessed by a sheerly creative urge:

> . . . sometimes I would feel myself connected to the well inside me and then I broke loose. There would come into my whole body a feeling of passionate certainty. . . . Then I would stand the world of appearances on its head, would reach in and down, would destroy savagely and re-create—not for painting or precisely for Art with a capital A, but for this very concrete creation itself. (p. 102)

And as a person, he can pass judgment in the very depths of his being on the baseness of his enslavement to his sexual desire for Beatrice:

> Therefore the tickling pleasure, the little death shared or self-inflicted was neither irrelevant nor sinful but the altar of whatever shoddy temple was left to us. But there remained deep as an assessment of experience itself the knowledge that if this was everything it was a poor return for birth, for the shames and frustrations of growing up. (p. 108)

Nevertheless, Sammy can no more escape his secular self than he can deny the actuality of the divine when it invades his awareness. As a man who must live with the consciousness that he has fallen, Sammy is provided by Golding with none of the consolations associated with ordinary Christian experience. The central ethic that the novel proposes, though conditioned by Sammy's vision in the prison camp of a universe informed by the divine, seems to me cast by Golding in determinedly secular terms. The "order of things" in "the new world" that Sammy perceives outside him "depended on pillars," and "the substance of these pillars," he discovers,

> . . . was a kind of vital morality, not the relationship of a man to remote posterity nor even to a social system, but the relationship of individual man to individual man— once an irrelevance but now seen to be the forge in which all change, all value, all life is beaten out into a good or a bad shape. (p. 189)

The ethic requires Sammy to strive continuously toward self-transcendence through relating himself to others, but it offers us no encouragement to imagine him as achieving a release from the self. By representing Sammy's dilemma without palliating it all through *Free Fall*, Golding dramatizes the essential limitation of our condition as humans powerfully and faithfully.

1. *Free Fall*, a Harbinger Book (New York & Burlingame, 1962), p. 6; this is the edition to which I give page references in my text.

2. James Baker notices the difficulty that Golding faces in representing Sammy's incoherence: the author must mediate between reproducing that incoherence accurately and, conversely, structuring it for purposes of intelligibility (*William Golding*, p. 56). But I think Baker finds the novel less structured than I do, nearer to a reproduction of life which demonstrates at last for the reader that "patternlessness is the only pattern" (p. 58). Powerful support for Baker's view is contained in a public statement which he quotes by Golding, made the year before *Free Fall* was published, about the new book's dealing with "the patternlessness of life before we impose our patterns on it" (p. 56). Yet I

wonder whether Golding's remark may not be interpreted to mean simply that the novel offers no encompassing solution to Sammy's dilemma as limited man. Certainly that dilemma—Sammy's experience of being ultimately trapped within his guilty self, yet from time to time transcending it—is dramatized throughout the story and thus becomes, to my mind, the fundamental pattern informing the novel's meaning. Mark Kinkead-Weekes and Ian Gregor, who have written the most illuminating criticism of *Free Fall* that I know (*William Golding*, pp. 165–99), argue that the novel finally accords the reader an indication, at least, of a pattern of meaning which would reconcile the human with the divine. I shall be taking issue later on with their interpretation of Golding's conclusion, but I think they trace very helpfully the larger outlines of the story.

3. All readers would agree that Sammy's cry for help is soon followed, however puzzlingly, by his release from the prison cell and his altered view of the universe. Relatively few critics seem to feel, as I do, that Sammy shows himself at last prepared to betray his comrades. And I am alone in suggesting that Golding intends through the passage to superimpose Sammy's approach towards a deliverance from the self upon his movement towards the abysmally selfish act of betrayal.

4. Nick Shales shares several major qualities with Phanocles, the Greek inventor in the play *The Brass Butterfly* (London, 1958)—which is a reworking of Golding's earlier comic novella "Envoy Extraordinary" (1956) and was published by him in the year before *Free Fall* appeared. Like Nick, Phanocles is a determined rationalist who nevertheless passes his days "in a condition of ravished astonishment" (p. 22) at the "reasonable miracles" of the created world (p. 55), and like Nick, Phanocles idealistically envisions a society remade if man would only attend to the scientific operations of the universe—though the Greek also betrays at moments an irritation with others and an arrogance that are foreign to the saintly Nick. Because it is a comedy, of course, *The Brass Butterfly* affects us very differently than does *Free Fall*, generating a good deal of its fun through the clashes between an unworldly Phanocles (inventor of a steamship, an explosive, and the printing press) who declares his "gods" to be "Law, Change, Cause and Effect, Reason" (p. 63), the Roman Emperor, who is mildly superstitious, officially committed to pagan religious doctrine, yet extremely knowledgeable in human affairs, and Postumus, the pragmatic general devoted to exercising his power efficiently. But one of the chief differences between *The Brass Butterfly* and Golding's earlier version of the story in "Envoy Extraordinary"—a difference that brings the play nearer in subject matter to *Free Fall*—is the development by Golding

of the religious elements, one sign of this being the transformation of Phanocles' sister, Euphrosyne, from a girl whose loveliness is marred by a harelip into a beautiful girl who has been converted to Christianity. Another change from "Envoy Extraordinary" in *The Brass Butterfly* is Golding's elaboration of the narrative climax into the sort of muddle (though here managed comically) which seems to me the defining structural characteristic of *Free Fall*. Postumus, threatening to take over as Emperor, is killed when he inadvertently sets off the explosive of Phanocles, which has been armed by Euphrosyne: the Emperor regards the event as a miracle performed by Jupiter, to whom he has just been praying in form, and becomes therefore convinced that the pagan doctrines to which he has half-heartedly subscribed must indeed be true; Euphrosyne sees the miracle as the work of the Christian God, who has "guided" her to arm the explosive (p. 70) ; Phanocles understands the event as demonstrating his sister's "intelligent" behavior and the operation of "Cause and Effect" in the handling of explosives (pp. 70–71) .

5. In many ways Beatrice reminds one of Mary Lovell in *Pincher Martin,* who is also self-contained, socially conventional, drawn to the church, prudish, and possessed of a powerful physical attraction for Pincher Martin, who once describes her behavior as expressing "a mystery that was not there" (p. 148) —though Mary reacts to Martin's rape with a violence that Beatrice never displays. The similarity of the figures suggests that they comprise a type for Golding, and one suspects that the type affects the imagination of the author more forcibly than the created characters affect the reader.

V

The Spire

Thematically regarded, *The Spire* (1964) develops naturally out of *Free Fall*. For it traces the gradual discovery by Jocelin, Dean of the Cathedral Church of Our Lady, that his life—far from being informed by the religious, as he imagines—is and has been influenced by the secular at every point, which brings him, like Sammy Mountjoy, to call out for help from another; but by the close of the novel he appears to achieve a somewhat greater degree of freedom from the self than Sammy Mountjoy has, though still testifying to the riddle of the universe, and, unlike Sammy, he passes at last into death. Structurally, however, *The Spire* is more conventional than *Free Fall*. Although it exposes us for the most part to the inner life of Jocelin, the novel is not a first-person narrative: whereas *Free Fall* (or even *Pincher Martin* in its flashbacks) violates chronology in following the recollections that present themselves to the individual consciousness of the leading character, *The Spire* progresses in a straight line, focusing on the change in Jocelin as he thrusts past one obstacle after another, becoming ever more guiltily involved, to complete the building of the spire which he believes that God initially showed him in a vision. Golding's mode in this book seems even barer, more stringently condensed, than in *Pincher Martin*—in part because he represents Jocelin's inner life less circumstantially than Martin's—though at moments *The Spire* reveals a densely ambiguous texture like *Pincher Martin*'s. But *The Spire* resembles *Pincher Martin* mainly in that Golding organizes both works to some extent around a sequence of invasions of the self by an unwelcome knowledge: as the world of Martin's ego crumbles, bit by bit, when he keeps being forced to recognize the otherness of the universe, so Jocelin's illusions about the purity of his actions are undermined, little by little, by the growing awareness pressed upon him of his guilt. Indeed, the number of such sequences in *The Spire* allies the novel with *The Inheritors* or *Lord of the Flies,* where, as we have already seen, Golding relies heavily on carefully graded series of various kinds to structure his narrative, generate its drive, and make his meaning.

In the next section of this chapter, I shall be referring to some of the forms that govern the development of *The Spire,* but I want to dwell primarily on the changes that slowly manifest themselves in Jocelin, for these seem to me the essence of the story's structure and theme. After that, I shall take up several characters and motifs employed by Golding to highlight what goes on in Jocelin. Then, to indicate Golding's verbal manner in this book, I shall examine a few of those oblique and ambiguous passages which record Jocelin's invasion by thoughts and feelings whose significance he resists recognizing. And finally I shall turn to the closing pages of *The Spire* in order to explore their meaning and comment on the story's theme.

On the simplest narrative level, Golding shapes his story through describing the construction of a spire for a church in medieval England and the realizations that it leads to in Dean Jocelin, the prime mover in the enterprise. As the novel begins, the job is getting underway, and we follow it through its increasingly threatening stages: the discovery that the ground below the crossways provides no proper foundation for such a structure; the moving of the earth in the pit beneath as the tower rises; the ringing of the stones in the church because of the added weight; the building of pinnacles and the encircling of the tower with a steel band, some 250 feet up, to contain the thrust on the pillars below; the swaying of the tower; the bending of the pillars by the crossways, which causes the master builder himself (Roger

Mason) to quit the job; the placing of the capstone and its supporting cone, which wrenches the spire from the perpendicular; and Jocelin's driving of a Holy Nail, during a wild storm, at the top of the spire to complete and preserve it. The spire built, Jocelin finds out, first, that he does not owe his preferment in the church to being a man "chosen" by God,[1] as he has believed, but to being the nephew of the worldly Alison, mistress to the former king. Then the very quality of the vision in which he felt the spire originally revealed to him by God is called in question by Father Adam, who ministers to him in the Dean's physical and spiritual weakness. Jocelin proceeds to seek forgiveness from Father Anselm, a friend of his youth who bitterly resents Jocelin's rise in the church, and from Roger Mason, one of several persons whom Jocelin has in effect destroyed because of his obsession with the spire; but on leaving Roger's room, the Dean is set upon by the people of the town, whom he has alienated through the building of the spire. On his deathbed, after deciding that *"There is no innocent work. God knows where God may be"* (p. 214), Jocelin suddenly sees the spire once more as a work of God, *"like the apple tree,"* and is overwhelmed by a sense of "terror and joy" as he expires (p. 215).

A résumé such as I have just given cannot begin to suggest the complexities that evolve from this basic narrative line, complexities so controlled by Golding that they themselves serve to shape the developing story, and here I can only indicate some of the more important ones. Thus the spire is both a physical fact in the external world and a presence within Jocelin himself, a presence that he sometimes experiences as a demonstration of his utter will and sometimes feels as realized in his very back, which slowly weakens as the building rises; the stones of the church actually sing and its pillars really bend, but often the singing occurs inside the head of Jocelin and the supports within him are menaced as the pressure mounts; the literal spire expresses Jocelin's extraordinary faith and absolute folly; a presence in the sky and a symbol of prayer to God, it stands over the pit at the crossways, the location of almost every evil happening in the novel; as a structure, the spire is at once a miracle and a menace; it testifies to Jocelin's faith, and it is associated, repeatedly, with the male organ. The course of Jocelin's experience in *The Spire* may also be viewed as a continuing assault by the secular on the self, which struggles more and more desperately to resist the awareness that invades it until it is finally overpowered. At the start of the book, the spiritually assured Jocelin welcomes the presence of Roger Mason's workers in the church despite the chaos they bring, although he is irritated at moments by their worldliness; after he has begun to intuit dimly his own guilt, he tries to escape from the world by busying himself up in the spire, thus withdrawing as well ever more firmly from his responsibilities as dean and from his colleagues in the church; when he climbs to drive the Holy Nail, he imagines the storm as a host of devils let loose to destroy the spire, although morally speaking, Jocelin is by this time beset by a multitude of hints concerning his own sins; after the completion of the spire, as his awareness of guilt grows, Jocelin becomes increasingly humble, groping his way back into the world of men which he has forsaken and struggling to come to terms both with the knowledge of himself which has been thrust upon him and with the final manifestation of the divine. This particular line of development in *The Spire* is also dramatized by Golding through a series of visitations of Jocelin: first, by a "guardian angel" who warms him (p. 18), reinforcing Jocelin's conviction that God approves the building of the spire;

then, by this angel alternating with the Devil, who keeps assailing Jocelin with lurid sexual visions; later, by a combination of angel and devil at one point where Jocelin realizes much of what he stands responsible for and willingly assents to his punishment, "Then his angel put away the two wings from the cloven hoof and struck him from arse to the head with a white-hot flail" (p. 181); after that, by a "dark angel" (p. 190); and finally, by "a cloud of angels flashing in the sunlight" that he sees, near the end of the book, when looking at an apple tree, the angels a miraculous transformation of its blooms (p. 196).

But Jocelin's gradual progress towards self-knowledge is the fundamental substance of the narrative in *The Spire*, and as such worth tracing in more detail. The first two chapters of the novel present a Jocelin extremely confident of his mission while they also contain several indications of his frailties. About the world of the church he feels almost divinely omniscient, chuckling over how well he knows the people in it, "what they are doing and will do . . . what they have done" (p. 4), although he cautions himself rather coyly to "remember that the spire isn't everything" (p. 5) and a little later proclaims his humility, *"Lord, I thank Thee that Thou hast kept me humble"* (p. 18). In fact, of course, he readily allies himself with the divine: he overhears one deacon remarking to another, "He thinks he is a saint! A man like that!" (p. 9), though Jocelin does not realize that the men are speaking of him; he imagines that a head of him being sculptured by the dumb man, which seems primarily intended to capture his physical likeness, represents him as "an angel," if not the "Holy Spirit" (p. 20); he even identifies himself with God when addressing Roger Mason, "I shall thrust you upward by my will. It's God's will in this business" (p. 35). His certainty of being chosen to oversee the construction of the spire begins immediately to affect his personal relationships: when Pangall, who is in charge of keeping the church clean, weeps in telling how the builders mock his impotence, Jocelin is made impatient by the tears, his "irritation" disappearing as he ignores Pangall to look up at the "empty air" that the spire will occupy (p. 16); Father Adam he depersonalizes into a man with "no face" whom he calls "Father Anonymous" (p. 22); he dismisses a letter from Alison—an aunt who hopes to arrange for her burial in the church—because he has already gotten money from her for the spire; despite a surge of friendliness toward Father Anselm, who has quarreled with him rather nastily about the spire, the Dean exerts his authority in requiring the Sacrist to stand watch over the workmen at the crossways and thus severs "the frayed thread that bound them" together (p. 31), though after a while—when "Buoyed up by his joy" at the news that a Holy Nail is to be sent from Rome —Jocelin offers Anselm a "release . . . from this duty" (p. 44). When the Dean is annoyed at sensing opposition to the job in someone else, he suspects the other of regarding the spire as "Jocelin's Folly" (pp. 15, 31), but his assurance is scarcely shaken. If Roger shows him that a proper foundation is lacking, the Dean chides him for unwillingness "to believe in a miracle" and then accuses the master builder of temporizing in order to keep his crew together before departing to find work somewhere else (pp. 34–35). Only once in these first two chapters does the secular begin to infringe on Jocelin's awareness, in a typically oblique passage. He has been asking Roger why the workers "pick on" Pangall—whose impotence, as it later turns out, the Dean fully realizes and whose wife Jocelin has desired for years. When Roger glances at him, "Jocelin felt the fluttering of a dozen things behind his lips that he might have given sound to, if it had not been for the dark eyes looking so directly into his. It was like standing on the edge of something" (p. 38) ; and the last sentence links the knowledge that Jocelin resists with the pit, which comes to figure so prominently in the story as an image of the burgeoning secular life that he wishes to repress.

In the chapters that follow, the facts and feelings which infringe on Jocelin's consciousness multiply and become more defined, so he must struggle harder to withstand them as he pushes on with the work. The builders he continues to transform from persons into "his instruments . . . people he had to use . . . little more than apes" (p. 50), and we also learn how Jocelin has secured timbers for his spire through arranging for an almost illiterate young fellow "to be made a canon," who then "went back to his hunting" (pp. 66–67). But he is startled to discover that Pangall's wife and Roger Mason are irrevocably attracted to each other, caught up "in some sort of tent that shut them off from all other people, and he saw how they feared the tent, both of them, but were helpless" (p. 52). When Pangall interprets Jocelin's gesture with a model of the spire as a jibe at the sweeper's impotence, thus reminding the Dean of the sexual and of Goody Pangall, Jocelin yearns for "the purity of the light" but instead finds himself "looking down at the tiles of the floor with their heraldic beasts" (p. 57), and the thought bursts into his mind that the presence of Goody Pangall will keep Roger on the job. The thought is "so allaying" because it assures Jocelin that the work will go on, but "so terrible" because it places Goody Pangall within a sexual orbit, albeit Roger's (p. 59). That night, Satan visits Jocelin for the first time, torturing him with what the Dean attempts to protect himself by thinking "a meaningless and hopeless dream" in which Jocelin lies "crucified," jeered at, and in which Goody is disguised as "Satan himself, rising out of the west, clad in nothing but blazing hair . . . tormenting him so that he writhed" (pp. 59–60). He tries to evade the dream by becoming "very busy" (p. 61) and by telling himself, "I am about my Father's business" (p. 62). But at times "a dark corner of his mind surprised him"—on the sight of Roger or either of the Pangalls—and he is forced to say, "There's much more to come," though he claims that the words have "no logical meaning" (p. 70). Although he is terrified at the moving of the earth in the pit—"Some form of life; that which ought not to be seen or touched, the darkness under the earth" (p. 74)—he remains determined that the construction proceed, asserting the purity of his own "faith" and "vision" when Roger argues that the building should stop (pp. 79–80). In the face of Roger's intention to leave, Jocelin discloses that he has written a letter to prevent Roger from getting work at Malmesbury (p. 82); betrays the fact that he will use Roger's attraction to Pangall's wife as a lever to keep the master builder on the job (p. 81); indeed, reveals obliquely his willingness to sacrifice even the woman whom he does not know he loves, "I would protect her if I could" (p. 81). When Roger, frightened both by the impossibility of the job and by his growing involvement with Goody Pangall, begs Jocelin to release him "for the love of God," the Dean refuses, knowing that Roger "will never be the same man again" (p. 83). At the very moment when he realizes his "decision" to thrust on with the structure, however, Jocelin feels "a kind of sick apprehension, not because the spire was in danger; but because the spire was not in danger" (p. 82)—because, in short, he vaguely intuits the guilt of behaving as he does. The immediate consequence of his decision is the scene at the crossways in which Jocelin watches the rioting workers, tormenting Pangall once more, pursue

him like a "pack" of animals and sees Goody Pangall standing in a torn dress while she and Roger wordlessly acknowledge, looking at each other across the pit, how absolutely they
are bound together. Then the arms of the dumb man, who is
shielding the Dean with his body, "leapt apart" (p. 85), and
Jocelin collapses under the weight of the crowd, an indication of the degree to which he is burdened by his increasing
awareness of the secular.

Now Jocelin seeks to lose himself in the constructing of the
spire, cultivating his "indifference" to the people around
him (p. 93), but the "high laugh" that repeatedly breaks
from him marks the strain he is under (p. 88). If he stands
in the crossways and gazes up at the tower, the brightness
compels him to look down at the floor with its filth, which
makes him think vexedly of Pangall (who has disappeared)
and also contains "a twig . . . with a rotting berry" that
triggers "a whole train of memories and worries and associations" in the Dean's mind (pp. 89–90) —though not until
much later does Jocelin fully realize that Pangall lies mur-
dered in the pit "with a sliver of mistletoe between his ribs"
(p. 204). He is "irked" by Goody Pangall, though he pro-
fesses to feel "nothing about her but compassion" for the
"shame" he attributes to her at being deserted by her husband (p. 94). But she actually avoids him because she senses,
and has always sensed, his physical attraction to her, as is
clear when she replies to his "My child, you are very dear to
me" with "Not you *too!*" (p. 95). Driven by his "incomprehension" of these words, Jocelin determines to "Work!
Work!" and escapes once more to the spire (p. 95). But even
while he tries to concentrate on it, kneeling aloft in the
tower, "unlooked-for things came with the spire," and he can
only think dumbly, "Have mercy. Or teach me"—"But there
was no answer" (p. 100). At the news that Goody is preg-

nant, "A great anger swamped Jocelin" and then "tears streamed" from his eyes, but he retains self-control enough to offer fraudulent thanks to God, "these are tears of joy because Thou hast remembered Thy handmaiden" (p. 105).

Engaging himself again in overseeing the construction of the spire, Jocelin treats Roger more outrageously than ever. He is so "impaled on his will" (p. 109) that he rejects a new plea for "mercy" from Roger (p. 110), and he then lectures the master builder, with apparent humility, on the fact that they are both like "mayfly," transitory and ignorant beings, but the source of what he preaches is his "will" to complete the spire (p. 111). When Roger describes his fears for the structure so graphically that the Dean is compelled to live through in his imagination the fall of the spire, Jocelin persists in regarding this as a plot on Roger's part to stop the building and goes on to declare that both of them have been chosen for the work, that the spire is not his own "Folly" but "God's," from Whom "comes the command to do what makes no sense at all"—yet these words issue from the "Voice of the devouring Will, my master" (p. 116), which Jocelin refers to as if it were divine, though the phrasing suggests that this "Will" is in truth his own. He even tries to pressure Roger by adverting to the master builder's moral terror at submitting to the charms of Goody Pangall, to which Roger responds by calling Jocelin "The devil himself" (pp. 117–18). Appropriately enough, the Dean shortly finds Roger and Goody together in the spire, and as a result of this proof that they have made love,

> . . . the memories came storming in—a green girl running in the close and slowing decorously for my Lord the Dean, my Reverend Father, the shy smile and the singing of the child's game, noticed, approved, and at last looked

for, yes looked for, expected, cherished, a warmth round
the heart, an unworldly delight, the arranged marriage
with the lame man, the wimpled hair, the tent. . . . (p.
121)

The associations indicate that the Dean can still manage to
consider his own relationship with Goody Pangall in the past
as uncontaminated by any sexual attraction, but the mention of "the arranged marriage" with the impotent Pangall
betrays for the first time how Jocelin has sought practically
to preserve her for himself.

Rededicating himself to "Work! Work! Work!" (p. 122),
he attempts to put to rest the images of Goody Pangall that
haunt him by writing to arrange for her to be taken into a
religious house at Stilbury. And then he becomes conscious
that the tower itself sways in the air, a reflection for the
reader of Jocelin's moral vacillation. For on learning the
terms of the abbess, his "first thought" is "that Stilbury was
too near," an indication that he would resist the attractions
of Goody, but his "second thought," "more confused," is that
"Stilbury was quite far enough," which expresses his desire
to hold on to Goody if he can (p. 129). Shortly, however, she
is discovered with Roger by the master builder's wife, and,
when Jocelin comes on the scene to tell her of his plan with
money in his hand, the pregnant Goody suspects him of
intending sexual advances, goes into labor, and dies—
though Jocelin cherishes the illusion that she has thought
him simply an "accuser" from "the church" (p. 131).

After the death of Goody Pangall, Jocelin is invaded more
and more powerfully by an awareness of the secular, which
forces him at times to see himself with gradually increasing
clarity, although he remains committed to finishing the
spire. Conscious now and then "of a feeling rising in him

. . . like a level of dark water" (p. 133), Jocelin can "try"—
if he closes his mind to the "golden maze" that he associates
with Goody—"to examine the extraordinary tides of feeling
that were swallowing him up" (p. 141). But the "proposi-
tions" that he articulates are formulas which do not take full
account of his personal involvement, and "the spire in his
head prevented him from coming to a conclusion" about
them (p. 141). Once, when he is remembering his earlier
years as if they were "another life," he suddenly thinks
"There was God!" and then asks himself (as I understand
the passage) whether that thought is "included" in his present existence—"But there was no answer. . . . And then the
spire put the thoughts out of his head" (p. 142). After Roger
has quit the job and Jocelin's "will," declaring itself among
"flames of love" for the workers, has "promised them more
money" to complete the task (pp. 146–47), the Dean one day
finds himself alone in the spire and confronts, in a metal
sheet, a true reflection of his physical self: "He knelt and
peered in at the wild halo of hair, the skinny arms and legs
that stuck out of a girt and dirty robe" (p. 149). He begins
to relate this reflection to the terrible events that have transpired since he saw the rioting workers, Goody Pangall, and
Roger together at the crossways, but he still clings to the
purity of his original vision concerning the spire: "Well,
Jocelin, this is where we have come. It began when we were
knocked down, I think. . . . We can remember what happened since then, but what happened before is some sort of
dream. Except for the vision" (p. 150). When a commission
of the church arrives to judge whether the Dean, who has
been so obsessed with the spire, is fit to retain his position,
Jocelin freely admits that the others think him mad, confessing "Perhaps I am" (p. 163), and also affirms, "All I know is,
I looked for men of faith to be with me; and there was none"

(p. 159) . While struggling to explain himself to the commission, nevertheless, Jocelin cannot elude the encroachment of the secular, referring obliquely both to Goody Pangall (ironically, the commission believes that the "she" he speaks of is "Our Lady") and to the dead Pangall, "built in" under the crossways (p. 159) . And when at last he drives the Holy Nail to complete the spire, a deed which he has hoped will free him, images of Goody rush in on his exhausted self: he thinks of her first as a child whom he has "stood looking down on . . . loving her innocence and beauty"; but then he envisions her as a naked female presence (undisguised, for the first time in the novel) to whom he makes love—though Jocelin still places the latter vision in the "uncountry" of his mind, where the two act with "no sin," thus still shielding himself to some degree from acknowledging the reality of her attraction for him (p. 171) .

But this "new knowledge" with which Jocelin has been visited is by no means the final stage in his self-discovery. During a talk with Alison he learns that, far from being chosen by God for advancement in the church, he has been chosen by his aunt, who has suggested to the former king, after a sexual encounter, that he forward the career of her nephew as a kind of joke. Alison even questions the gift of the Holy Nail, hinting that the person who sent it to Jocelin wanted to avoid giving hard cash. Yet she is frightened at his reaction to what she has said and so agrees with him that the continued "haunting" of Jocelin by Goody Pangall must be "witchcraft" (pp. 179–80) —though Jocelin himself, on his aunt's departure, feels that "There's a pattern" in whatever has happened and that "There's more to be destroyed" (p. 180) . His prediction is fulfilled in part as he is led once more to the crossways, where he abases himself spiritually as well as physically, again obliquely acknowledging the murder of

Pangall, and is "struck . . . with a white-hot flail" by his dark angel (p. 181). But he has yet to learn that his initial vision itself of the spire is suspect. The record of the experience— set down some years earlier—that he has Father Adam read aloud is full of phrases about Jocelin's "certainty and abnegation," "my nothingness in this scheme," "my new-found humility and new-found knowledge" (pp. 185–86), but the vision seems to have had its origin in a mere "feeling" that "rose from my heart" (p. 184), and Father Adam maintains that Jocelin's prayer for the spire is no more than a prayer of the second level ("where we are given an encouragement, a feeling, an emotion"—but not, presumably, accorded a real vision) : "Your prayer was a good prayer certainly; but not very" (p. 190). Nevertheless, even though Jocelin alludes to his involvement with Goody Pangall—"It must be witchcraft; otherwise how could she and he come so flatly between me and heaven?"—Father Adam first prays for him, then "smiled" at Jocelin, apparently forgiving him for his humanity; and "at once" Jocelin sees Father Adam as a distinctive person to whom he cries out, "Help me," his call releasing in Jocelin "an infinite sea of grief which . . . overflowed liberally at his eyes" (p. 189).

Now he can set about making his peace with the world to which he has returned. Although an interview with Father Anselm brings him to realize that the man whom he used to think his friend has always been rather contemptuous of Jocelin's feelings, envies his rise in the church, and indeed regards him as a Satan who has led the chapter spiritually astray, Jocelin begs Anselm to "Forgive me for being what I am," but Anselm simply departs when asked whether he does really "feel" forgiveness (p. 195). After experiencing the miraculous vision of an apple tree on his way to confront Roger Mason, who hates the Dean for oppressing him during

the building of the spire, Jocelin strips off his religious attire
to kneel before Roger, presenting himself as an erring
human who acknowledges most of his guilt—"Once you said
I was the devil himself. It isn't true. I'm a fool. . . . I'm a
building with a vast cellarage where the rats live. . . . I
injure everyone I touch, particularly those I love. Now I've
come in pain and shame, to ask you to forgive me" (p.
202) —and Roger embraces him. But Roger's forgiveness is
short-lived, for there is still a "formless" mass in Jocelin's
head that he seeks to express, a residue of guilt which, as he
articulates it, turns Roger against him once more. One part
of this "formless thing" is the muddle that now, for Jocelin,
characterizes the spire itself:

"You see it *may* be what we were meant to do, the two of
us. . . . So I gave it my body. What holds it up, Roger? I?
The Nail? Does she, or do you? Or is it poor Pangall,
crouched beneath the crossways, with a sliver of mistletoe
between his ribs?" (p. 204)

When Jocelin follows up the reference to Pangall (whom
Roger has killed) by saying, "So there's still something you
can do, Roger my son," the master builder interprets him as
threatening blackmail.[2] What Jocelin actually wants from
Roger, however, is a perverse assurance about the nature of
Goody Pangall, another part of "the formless thing in his
head." For if Roger can testify that Goody "knew" of or
"even consented to" the murder of her husband, that would
prove her a witch and thus enable Jocelin still to ward off
the realization that the attraction he has felt for her is
sheerly secular in origin, the desire of a mere man for a
woman (p. 205). Although he evades complete knowledge
of himself, one measure of Jocelin's spiritual effort here is

the fact that "something out of my control" (p. 204) has made him ask for this assurance about Goody from Roger, which indicates that he is devoting his energies to seeing himself as clearly as he may; and he goes on to admit, before Roger throws him out, that "I sacrificed her too. Deliberately" to the constructing of the spire, that, by later appearing at her door, "I killed her as surely as if I'd cut her throat" (p. 206). On his way back to the church, however, he is hunted down by the people of the town just as Pangall (for whose shame and death Jocelin bears a share of the responsibility) was hunted down by the workers, and the weight of the world smashes down on his back, this time unprotected by the arms of the dumb man.

In the closing chapter of *The Spire,* Jocelin lies suspended between life and death, periodically aware of the secular, his body, and his guilt as well as of the spiritual, judging himself and others, yet remaining confronted with the riddle of himself and the universe, a riddle not to be resolved by the understanding of a limited human being. Informed that Roger has attempted suicide (because he fears specifically the revelation of Pangall's death, I assume, though Roger also knows himself to be a ruined man professionally—and he has been broken morally by his relation with Goody Pangall), Jocelin "felt the weight" of his responsibility for the master builder, for the others whom he has wronged, and for the spire; yet he also thinks, "I can't even feel for them. Or for myself" (p. 212)—ambiguous words which, even if they suggest that in his exhausted state Jocelin lacks compassion for others, also declare that he has no pity for himself. While he is compelled to realize that the "witchcraft" of Goody Pangall still haunts him, he nevertheless tries to ease the "anxious" Father Adam, to whom he "desired to give . . . something," by allowing the Father to believe that Jocelin's mention of a pagan Berenice (with hair as beautiful as Goody's) is a reference to a Christian saint (p. 213). He can see the whole world as inhabited by people stripped down to their physical selves who yet, in their arrogance as humans, "pace or prance in sheets of woven stuff"; and, though he judges them by thinking, *"How proud their hope of hell is,"* he also judges himself in recognizing that *"There is no innocent work. God knows where God may be"* (p. 214). Then, before being granted his final vision of the spire prior to dying, Jocelin can acknowledge it to be "a stone hammer" on which he has expended "four people" (p. 214).

To rehearse the development of Jocelin so elaborately as I have is to indicate, I trust, how prevailingly *The Spire* concentrates on his inner life and perhaps to suggest that many of Golding's characters here live less in their own right than as adumbrations of the Dean. Thus he is juxtaposed on the one hand to the petty, legalistic, unforgiving Father Anselm and on the other to the naïve but forgiving Father Adam. Goody Pangall keeps betraying by her avoidance of Jocelin an intuition of that sexual drive in him which he masks as a spiritual concern for her. Pangall himself is paralleled to the Dean in that both are regarded by the workers as foolish persons who may keep off bad luck (pp. 38, 145), both are impotent in their different ways, and both are hunted down by a riotous crowd. The commission of the church which relieves the Dean of his duties serves to set off the simplicity of Jocelin and to place him in a relatively winning light, for, though it views some of his statements with favor, it appears narrowly moralistic in deciding against him because he has not always considered the workers to be wicked men and because he has long since abandoned confessing to Father Anselm. Incidentally, the sudden arrival of the commission as the obsessed Jocelin searches for the Holy Nail, "racing" to drive it in before "the Devil" can destroy the spire (p. 154), seems to me an instance of the risk Golding runs in focusing our attention so continually on the workings of Jocelin's mind, since our translation into the outer world is shockingly abrupt and its figures are pale in comparison with the presences that haunt Jocelin.[3] Probably the most fully developed of the major characters, other than the Dean, is Roger Mason, who at many moments emerges as a person with a life of his own, yet even he is used by Golding to highlight certain features of Jocelin. The master builder testifies repeatedly to the folly of building the spire, a fact which Jocelin often wishes to gloss over; Roger is quite aware of Goody Pangall's attraction for him and strives to resist it, whereas Jocelin's struggle to resist Goody's attractions takes a different form; Roger, in his guilt, seeks to hide the death of Pangall from the world, while Jocelin, guilty in his own way of killing Pangall, would conceal the death from himself; and as Roger remains a limited human to the end, marked by his responsibility for Pangall's death, so Jocelin remains subject to the lingering illusion—generated by the self as a fraudulent protector of its innocence—of Goody Pangall's "witchcraft."

If Roger Mason is, aside from the Dean, Golding's most rounded character in *The Spire,* the most purely symbolic is surely the dumb man, who is to be associated in various ways with the physical self that Jocelin keeps straining to repress. This powerfully masculine figure is described in greater physical detail than any other character in the novel (pp. 18–19), and, as we have already noted, he is engaged in sculpturing four heads of Jocelin to be set in the spire, heads which appear to reproduce the Dean's features accurately, but which Jocelin converts into expressions of his own spiritual power (pp. 19–20). It is the dumb man who takes Jocelin to the crossways to see the earth moving in the pit, that image—for the Dean—of a "form of life . . . which ought not to be seen or touched" (p. 74). (Significantly, the stone heads are at first thrown into the pit, then later re-moved—after the riot at the crossways—as Jocelin persists in trying to repress the dawning awareness of his guilt.) And it is the dumb man who attempts to shield the Dean's body from the crowd of workers, but whose "arms leapt apart" under the weight of this assault by the physical world on Jocelin (p. 90). When Jocelin tells the workmen, after the pillars in the church have begun to bend, that he intends ultimately to preach from a pulpit built in the crossways, they think the person who would do so "a fool," "But the dumb man came to Jocelin, humming and nodding and tapping himself on the chest" (pp. 148–49). The sentence allies the two men and suggests that Jocelin is as trapped within his physical self as the dumb man is, a fact which renders the Dean, too, essentially inarticulate so long as he represses the consciousness of his secular self. The "naked" Goody Pangall who invades the "uncountry" of Jocelin's mind, after he has driven the Holy Nail, is described as "humming from an empty mouth" (p. 178), a phrase that links her to the dumb man and the physical actuality with which he is associated. Farther on in the novel, the dumb man leads Jocelin to the crossways once more to show him the "rubble" within the pillars which the Dean has always imagined to be perfect because they were erected by the "giants" who first built the church (p. 181). Finally, as Jocelin lies on his deathbed acknowledging what he has been and is, he himself summons the dumb man to sculpture a figure, "without ornament," of his wasted body for the tomb (p. 211).[4] Thus the dumb man is employed at point after point in the story to chart Jocelin's resistance to and developing acknowledgment of his physical self.

As the other characters in *The Spire* function primarily to illuminate Jocelin, so do the motifs which Golding creates in his narrative. We have already noticed the multiple meanings relevant to Jocelin that accrue as Golding elaborates on the spire, and my many references to the crossways indicate that it is a similarly complex vehicle for representing the muddled condition of Jocelin. But the only motif that I shall isolate here is the bough of mistletoe that appears in the story both as the literal instrument of Pangall's death and as an image of the burgeoning awareness in Jocelin of the secular. (Quite aside from the novel, mistletoe has a rich range of implications: it is sacred, protects one against witchcraft, promotes fertility, and is associated with sacrificial killing.) On its first manifestation in the book, mistletoe is not even named. Standing in the crossways shortly after the riot of the workers there and the disappearance of Pangall, Jocelin looks at the filth on the floor about "a clear space . . . where the paving was replaced over the pit," immediately wonders testily *"Where is Pangall,"* and sees "a twig lying across his shoe, with a rotting berry that clung obscenely to the leather," which he tries to shake from his foot (pp. 89–90). The phrasing itself here is portentous; moreover, the sight of the twig releases "a whole train of memories and worries and associations" which Jocelin at this moment can think "altogether random," although they include a "vision of the spire warping and branching and sprouting" that fills him with "terror" (p. 90). Much later, as the pressure mounts on him after Goody Pangall's death, Roger's defection from the job, and the temporary desertion by the workers to participate in the pagan ceremonies of Midsummer Night, Jocelin stares down from the spire "to a pit

dug at the crossways like a grave made ready for some nota-
ble," remembers seeing there the "twig with a brown, obscene berry" that "lay against his foot," and whispers "Mistletoe!" (p. 151) —but cannot yet allow himself to realize
that the grave is Pangall's and that his death is a fact for
which the Dean himself must share responsibility. In trying
to explain himself to the commission, Jocelin first mentions
"the mistletoe berry" without elucidating further (p. 160),
then settles on the plant as an image of the "complications"
with which his "work" of completing the spire is beset: "A
single green shoot at first, then clinging tendrils, then
branches, then at last a riotous confusion—" (p. 162). And
this is the image that he comes back to, while talking with
Father Adam, in his stumbling efforts to describe his own
guilty involvement in the whole project, which includes
"More than you can ever know. Because I don't really know
myself. Reservations, connivances. The work before everything. And woven through it, a golden thread—No. Growth
of a plant with strange flowers and fruit, complex, twining,
engulfing, destroying, strangling" (p. 187) —though Jocelin's refusal to pursue the image of the "golden thread"
shows him still repressing his thoughts of Goody Pangall. As
for the literal mistletoe, he can identify it explicitly with
Pangall's death—for us and for himself—only in his final
scene with Roger, where Jocelin struggles once more to articulate the "formless" mass in his mind as he advances toward
self-knowledge (p. 204).

Clearly Golding orders the references to mistletoe—as he
manages the other motifs in *The Spire,* or the motifs in his
earlier books, for that matter—in such a way that they gradually accumulate meaning as well as narrative pressure. The
same sort of meticulous gradation, as I have already argued,

characterizes the invasions of Jocelin by the secular that recur throughout the story. But I turn to three of these invasions now in order primarily to demonstrate what seems to me the most typical mode of Golding's prose in this novel. Despite the fact that many of Dean Jocelin's thoughts and expressions are religiously oriented, Golding does not create in his writing here anything like the religious aura that we saw him achieve at times in *Free Fall* through a variety of Biblical echoes. And, while Jocelin's resistance to the assaults of the world may remind us of Pincher Martin's to the assaults of the other on his ego, the Dean's inner life is rendered in much less detail than Martin's: which is to say that the oblique significances of Jocelin's thoughts are more easily grasped by the reader, that the controlling ambiguity of the spiritual and the secular is more sharply defined, that the prose of *The Spire* is essentially barer in mode than the prose of *Pincher Martin*.

The first passage describes Jocelin's reaction just after he has initially become aware of the mutual attraction binding Goody Pangall to Roger Mason and imagined them enclosed in a "tent that shut them off from all other people" (p. 52). The Dean responds by passing moral judgment on the world around him, but the imagery reveals that he is more deeply implicated with Goody Pangall than he yet realizes:

Then an anger rose out of some pit inside Jocelin. He had glimpses in his head of a face that drooped daily for his blessing, heard the secure sound of her singing in Pangall's kingdom. He lifted his chin, and the word burst out over it from an obscure place of indignation and hurt.

"No!"

All at once it seemed to him that the renewing life of the world was a filthy thing, a rising tide of muck, so that he gasped for air, saw the gap in the north transept and hurried through it into what daylight there was. Immediately he heard the distant jeering of men, workmen; and, at that temperature of feeling, understood what an alehouse joke it must seem to see the dean himself come hurrying out of a hole with his folly [a model of the spire] held in both hands. (p. 53)

The "face that drooped daily for his blessing" belongs to Goody Pangall, Jocelin thus testifying that in his view their relationship is purely spiritual. Yet a further irony lurks in his reference to the "sound of her singing" as "secure," for, as it later turns out, Jocelin has indeed tried to secure her from the world and for himself through marrying her to the impotent Pangall. The "indignation and hurt" that erupt in Jocelin's "No!" may express his moral outrage at the attachment between Goody and Roger, but they betray as well his personal jealousy of Roger, emerging as they do from "some pit inside Jocelin," the phrase allying their source with the actual pit beneath the crossways, which is for the Dean the location of all sorts of strange and unmanageable life. While he regards this "life of the world" as "a filthy thing" and tries to escape it, at his present "temperature of feeling" he can even understand that the workers interpret his posture with the model of the spire in sexual terms—though of course their idea seems blasphemous to the Dean.

In the course of the second passage, Jocelin comes a good deal closer to recognizing his guilt, yet he still resists acknowledging it completely, protecting himself, as it were, by referring at the close of the passage to a religious song, though its words have a secular relevance for the reader. Jocelin is striving to pray after being terrified at the sight of Goody Pangall in labor and after clutching once more at the notion that she has thought him merely her spiritual "accuser," though he has also admitted to God that he "consented" to the involvement of Roger and Goody in order to further the building of the spire, but his efforts at prayer are in vain.

> Then he forgot his knees, his hunger, forgot everything in a tumult of glimpses that presented themselves to him as if they were connected, though they had neither order nor logic. There was the arranged marriage and the swallow's nest. There was hair and blood, and a lame man with a broom limping through the crossways. He made no sense of these things, but endured them with moanings and shudderings. Yet like a birth itself, words came that seemed to fit the totality of his life, his sins, and his forced cruelty, and above all the dreadful glow of his dedicated will. They were words that the choir boys sang sometimes at Easter, quaint words; but now the only words that meant anything.
>
> *This have I done for my true love.* (p. 132)

The "glimpses" that invade Jocelin, of course, define the "logic" of his responsibility, though he cannot yet permit himself to comprehend how they are "connected." The "marriage" that he himself "arranged" to wall off Goody from the world has led to her physical surrender to Roger in the "swallow's nest," to the "blood" of the terrifying childbirth (as well as to Goody's subsequent death), and even to the death of the "lame" Pangall, who presents himself to the Dean's memory at this moment simply as a living figure standing over the place where he is in fact buried. If Jocelin can make "no sense of these things," nevertheless "words" do indeed come "like a birth itself": a spiritual "birth" in that he feels them somehow expressive of the guilt which he has begun to realize, but "birth" also alludes to the secular, to the process of physical life itself which Jocelin regards with such horror that he keeps trying to deny his own participation in it. So by the conclusion of the passage Jocelin's acknowledgment of all he has done remains incomplete, poised on the ambiguity of a religious song with secular implications: for the Dean, "my true love" apparently yet signifies his dedication to God, while for the reader the phrase underlines the nature of Jocelin's attraction to Goody Pangall.[5]

In the final episode to be considered, a new piece of worldly knowledge thrusts itself on Jocelin's consciousness, further clarifying his guilt for him, but he is primarily invaded here by a spiritual compulsion to atone for his sins as he understands them. He has just been proposing to Alison that his continuing vision of Goody Pangall *"must* be witchcraft"—though also declaring, rather illogically, that the vision "is a logical part of all that went before" (p. 179) — when he is taken to the crossways by the dumb man, who has "chiselled a little hole in the stone" of one pillar:

> Jocelin understood what he had to do. He took the chisel with its burred-over head out of the hole, lifted up an iron probe and thrust it in. It sank in, in, through the stone skin, grated and pierced in among the rubble with which the giants who had been on the earth in those days had filled the heart of the pillar.
>
> Then all things came together. His spirit threw itself down an interior gulf, down, throw away, offer, destroy utterly, build me in with the rest of them; and as he did this he threw his physical body down too, knees, face, chest, smashing on the stone.

> Then his angel put away the two wings from the cloven
> hoof and struck him from arse to the head with a white-hot
> flail. (p. 181)

The discovery of corruption in the earlier builders, who
have "filled the heart of the pillar" with "rubble," suddenly
illuminates for Jocelin the corruption in his own heart
which has informed the construction of the spire. In abasing
himself after "all things came together," he seeks to abandon
the spiritual arrogance that has marked him and welcomes,
appropriately enough, the punishment of "his physical
body" as well—though he cannot yet articulate specifically
the death of Pangall (to which he refers obliquely in the
phrase "build me in with the rest of them") and though he
will remain haunted by what he thinks the "witchcraft" of
Goody Pangall until the end of *The Spire*.

The prose in which Golding represents Jocelin's sight of
an apple tree, while on his way to ask Roger Mason's forgiveness, and the dying man's ultimate vision of the spire is
similarly condensed, combining in its own way the spiritual
with the secular, and relatively unadorned in comparison
with, say, Sammy Mountjoy's visions in *Free Fall*. But I turn
to those passages now because they are crucial to our understanding of the condition that Jocelin finally achieves and so
to the meaning of *The Spire*. The apple tree is essentially a
counterpart to the mistletoe, that image, for Jocelin, of the
terrifyingly pagan life force which has engendered all the
complications in the building of the spire. Just before he sees
the tree, he has felt for the first time the beauty of the
physical world, sensing "a freshness about the air that stirred
the grief in his chest," and, when he looks up, the apple tree

with its blossoms appears to him—significantly—as initially divine:

> There was a cloud of angels flashing in the sunlight, they were pink and gold and white; and they were uttering this sweet scent for joy of the light and the air. They brought with them a scatter of clear leaves, and among the leaves a long, black springing thing. His head swam with the angels, and suddenly he understood there was more to the apple tree than one branch. It was there beyond the wall, bursting up with cloud and scatter, laying hold of the earth and the air, a fountain, a marvel, an apple tree. . . .
> (p. 196)

Divine as the tree is for Jocelin, he also sees it as including the secular: the "long, black springing thing" is an image of nature's potency; the fact that "he understood there was more to the apple tree than one branch" makes the tree a living whole for him; and it lays "hold" of both "earth" and "air." In short, the apple tree manifests a miraculous totality.

Towards the end of the novel, as we have already observed, the wasted Jocelin has progressed about as far as he can in judging human existence and acknowledging his own guilt: *"There is no innocent work. God knows where God may be."* When Father Adam declares his intention "to help" the dying man "into heaven," Jocelin's thought evidences the humility that he has attained, "And what is heaven to me unless I go in holding him by one hand and her by the other?" (p. 214) —unless, that is, he can feel that the Roger Mason and Goody Pangall whom he has destroyed are themselves forgiven and that he in turn is forgiven by them. On glancing up, Jocelin at first sees two eyes gazing back at him "which looked in, an eye for an eye, one eye for each eye" (pp. 214–15), but this perception—along with its allusion to a revengeful Jehovah—is transformed as "The two eyes slid together" to become a "window, bright and open," which reveals the spire against the sky:

> Round the division was the blue of the sky. The division was still and silent, but rushing upward to some point at the sky's end, and with a silent cry. It was slim as a girl, translucent. It had grown from some seed of rose-coloured substance that glittered like a waterfall, an upward waterfall. The substance was one thing, which broke all the way to infinity in cascades of exultation that nothing could trammel. (p. 215)

In the vision here accorded Jocelin, the spire, like the apple tree, unites the earth with the sky, is represented in imagery which combines the secular with the holy, appears to him as a substantial miracle. Overwhelmed by a mixture of "terror" and joyful "astonishment" at this transmutation of the evils that have gone into the construction of the spire, Jocelin exclaims, "Now—I know nothing at all," the sentence at once attesting to the personal humility which he has achieved and declaring all that a limited human can in the face of transcendent power. And when he is urged by Father Adam to perform some "gesture of assent," Jocelin can do no more than think, as he expires, *"It's like the apple tree!"* (p. 215)—words which identify the spire with the miraculous transformation of the natural, even if they also call up echoes of man's fall in Eden.

In thus emphasizing the miraculousness of the apple tree and of the spire as finally represented, I by no means wish to minimize the muddle which Jocelin experiences right up to the moment of dying. He is thoroughly bewildered at finding the "terror and joy" inseparably "mixed" within him. His last words, relating the spire to the apple tree, he cannot utter for Father Adam, and in any case they are for Jocelin "words of magic and incomprehension." Then, as if to underline the muddle of the human situation, Golding writes in the closing paragraph of the novel that the attentive Father Adam "could hear nothing," but "saw a tremor of the lips that might be interpreted as a cry of: *God! God! God!,*" and so "laid the Host on the dead man's tongue" (p. 215). Despite his insistence on this muddle, however, I think that Golding presents us in the closing pages of *The Spire* with a Jocelin whom we are to estimate rather differently than we do Sammy Mountjoy at the conclusion of *Free Fall.* For one thing, Sammy's decisive experience of the divine occurs halfway through the book and leaves him puzzled to the end, whereas Jocelin's truly miraculous visions, though they leave him confused, occur at the end of the story as the culmination of his progress towards acknowledging his guilt and attempting to lose himself: the spiritual development of Jocelin through *The Spire,* then, describes an arc quite unlike Sammy's course in *Free Fall.* The other crucial distinction, of course, is that Sammy remains alive at the conclusion of *Free Fall,* burdened with his awareness of his secular self, whereas Jocelin dies at the conclusion of *The Spire;* and, if one may project beyond Jocelin's death the spiritual advance that he has made through the pages of the story, one may imagine him as freed at last even from his lingering illusion about Goody Pangall's "witchcraft" and as finding himself forgiven.[6]

But to talk in this way about what may happen after Jocelin's death is to speculate about matters which the novel does not treat directly. What lies beyond question is the fact that in *The Spire* Golding represents the condition of living man to be as fundamentally limited as it was in *Free Fall*, as riddling to a sheerly human consciousness. Within the world of men as they are, the highest ideal that an enlightened Jocelin yearns to realize envisions no more than the interrelationship of the divine and the secular, "If I could go back, I would take God as lying between people and to be found there" (p. 212), an ideal that recalls the ethic of a "vital morality" informed by "love" which Sammy Mountjoy proposes in *Free Fall*. All of which is to say that in *The Spire*, as in *Free Fall*, Golding defines the condition of man as he sees it with rigorous honesty: he affirms the actuality of the divine in both novels, but the characters who experience it are not thereby enabled to transcend their secular selves—and so continue to reflect the limitations of us all.

1. *The Spire*, A Harvest Book (New York, 1964), p. 183; this is the edition to which I give page references in my text.

2. Mark Kinkead-Weekes and Ian Gregor attribute the killing of Pangall to the workmen rather than to Roger, and this interpretation may well be correct. I have assumed Roger himself to be the guilty party because his response to Jocelin's mention of the dead Pangall is so marked—as if the master builder fears a specifically personal disclosure (pp. 212–13). Although the details of the killing are obscured by Golding, certainly we are to imagine that Roger shares in the guilt for the deed—even if it is actually committed by his men—as fundamentally as does Jocelin in his own way.

3. My claim about the appearance of the commission is made more inclusively by Samuel Hynes, who finds that the results of Golding's concentration on the spire and Jocelin's mind are "a diminished sense of the actuality of the novel's physical world," a thinning of the other characters, and a paucity of "strong scenes," with "potentially powerful" ones being "treated sketchily" (*William Golding*, p. 45).

4. Oldsey and Weintraub misunderstand the significance of the dumb

man—and apparently the moral situation of Jocelin himself—in suggesting a relationship between Jocelin's preparations for his tomb and those of the speaker in Browning's "The Bishop Orders His Tomb at Saint Praxed's Church" (*The Art of William Golding*, pp. 141–42). Jocelin is humbly abandoning the world and accepting the corruption of his physical self, whereas the Bishop is arrogantly clinging to the world in his concern for the ornamentation of his tomb and indulging himself in every sensuous pleasure that offers itself to him or to his imagination.

5. Mark Kinkead-Weekes and Ian Gregor develop the ironies that inhere in Jocelin's quotation of the song: ". . . the words of the Easter carol refer directly to the betrayal of Christ, who sacrificed himself for love of fallen man, while Jocelin has both sacrified others and exploited their fall 'in the dreadful glow of his dedicated will.' Deeper still, and still hidden from Jocelin, the words carry a hint of the secret of his true feelings for this girl—a hinted betrayal not only of her, and of God, but of himself" (*William Golding*, p. 217).

6. Although he sketches Jocelin's advance toward self-knowledge, James Baker seems to me much too committed in his chapter on *The Spire* to placing the novel ultimately within a classical rather than a Christian context. He argues that the book is essentially a "tragedy," with Jocelin inhabiting "an Euripidean universe which is as ambiguous as his own soul" (*William Golding*, p. 71); that Jocelin "lives to discover the folly of his Christian illusions" (p. 71), his "uniquely Christian innocence" constituting his "tragic flaw" (p. 83); and that the "cosmos" shown Jocelin at the end of the story is "as unfathomable and mysterious as the one revealed to the heroes of Greek tragedy" (p. 72) —though Baker later acknowledges, in a sentence which strikes me as defining the mysteriousness of that cosmos in a different and truer fashion, that "No man could find the words to tell us what it is to see God" (p. 87). The critic keeps minimizing, I think, the fact that the self-awareness and humility towards which Jocelin moves are orthodox Christian virtues, demanding to be viewed as such in a novel so religiously oriented as *The Spire,* and that the universe revealed to Jocelin at the close of the book is "unfathomable" precisely because it evidences the miraculous, because it includes a Christian dimension. I am not thus hoping to claim, in opposition to Baker, that Golding is a doctrinal novelist, for, in examining both *Free Fall* and *The Spire,* I have been trying to insist that the experience of the divine by no means solves the problems of the central characters. Yet I believe that Golding does dramatize a view of man more conventionally Christian and human in one fundamental way than Baker will allow. In com-

menting on the "story" of man that the novelist tells in several of his works, Baker writes: "Into what kind of world do we awake if we survive spiritual adolescence and live on to look about us with a disillusioned eye? This is the fateful question which emerges from Golding's fiction. . . . Golding himself must finally admit us into the reality beyond innocence and ignorance" (p. 95). But the "reality beyond innocence"—the reality of fallen man who cannot escape his human condition so long as he lives—is exactly the subject of Golding's novels, and the "ignorance" against which Baker protests is exactly the mark of our limitations as secular beings, and so of Golding's candor as novelist.

VI

The Pyramid

One's immediate impressions on reading *The Pyramid* (1967) are of how radically it differs from its predecessors. There is almost nothing here, for instance, of the sustained narrative drive that characterizes *The Spire* or Golding's earliest books. Indeed, two sections of *The Pyramid* were first published separately, and Golding presents the three parts of the novel as relatively independent units—each one centering on the relationship between the narrator and a different character—although of course the three parts in combination illuminate each other and, in sequence, chart a particular development in the narrator. But the surface itself of *The Pyramid* reveals little of the tension and apparent complexity which mark, in their different ways, the earlier novels—in part because Golding's narrator in this book is rather muted as a character and often imperceptive. One more new feature is a number of essentially comic passages in the first half of *The Pyramid*, although through the last segment of the story the eccentric Bounce Dawlish, a music teacher who might be treated comically in another context, is in fact represented as the pathetic victim of her father and of the village in which she lives. But the chief difference between what has gone before and *The Pyramid* is that its materials do not create the impression of being as tightly structured and thematically oriented as those of the preceding novels. The complaint which we have seen lodged by some against Golding's earlier stories—that their fictional worlds are too rigidly cut to a pattern of meaning which every detail must serve—can hardly apply to *The Pyramid,* where Golding seems intent on fostering an illusion of actuality and fleshing out his world with gratuitous detail.

In some ways *The Pyramid* resembles *Free Fall:* both are first-person narratives with the adult protagonist looking back over his past; both employ oblique narrative structures;

both are set in twentieth-century England and place their narrators firmly in a social context. But the differences between the two are more striking than their similarities. Sammy Mountjoy is involved in an agonizing search for the moment when he lost his freedom, whereas Oliver—the main character in *The Pyramid*—describes a series of relationships in which he has participated, often rather observing others than projecting his own consciousness for us. Sammy, driven to discover some pattern by which he can understand himself, keeps analyzing his experiences; Oliver simply re-creates his with little retrospective commentary. A universe instinct with divinity is one fact of Sammy's experience in *Free Fall,* and the novel as a whole focuses on his personal condition as the guilty human which he has become. But the divine never manifests itself in *The Pyramid,* and this novel—instead of treating the interior of its central character in preeminently moral terms—explores the social environment as much as it does Oliver and shows him fundamentally conditioned as a person by that environment. While Sammy remains haunted from first to last by an awareness of the riddling intermixture of the divine and the secular which defines his existence, Oliver comes to realize only at the end of the book how thoroughly his life has been determined by that world which he has exhibited to us all along.

There is one important respect in which *The Pyramid* may be regarded as moving on thematically from Golding's previous novels. They have charted for us, in their various fashions, the moral consequences to man of being enclosed within himself; and *The Pyramid,* as I understand it, presents us with a man who recognizes finally the degree to which he is enclosed within himself. But the limiting condition for the individual highlighted in the earlier books is man's moral nature itself, whereas in *The Pyramid* the limiting condition seems to be the individual's social environment. In *The Spire,* we may remember, a Jocelin burdened by his sense of personal guilt thinks, "If I could go back, I would take God as lying between people and to be found there" (p. 212). The epigraph of *The Pyramid* refers directly to "love" rather than to God and offers it as the ideal that should inform the relations of the individual with his fellows: "*If thou be among people make for thyself love, the beginning and end of the heart.*" But the story portrays an individual so deeply influenced by the social facts and attitudes of the world he matures in that he cannot break out of himself decisively in any of the three personal relationships which he depicts for us, even though he becomes conscious of his failure at last.

What I have said about *The Pyramid*'s lowering of narrative tension, the circumstantiality of its represented life, and its concern with a rather ordinary subject matter might be construed as evidence that the book betrays a lapse in that imaginative vitality so characteristic of its predecessors. And such may indeed be the case, for certainly this story never grips us as forcibly as do Golding's earlier fictions. Yet we have already observed him radically shifting both his materials and his manner from novel to novel, and *The Pyramid* tempts one to view it as Golding's move into what is for him a new fictional terrain, the thoroughgoingly realistic novel. It might even be argued that the relative lack of narrative resonance in this story is expressive of Oliver's imperceptiveness, and that society in fact imposes its values on the ordinary individual so necessarily and indiscernibly that at least one accurate way of dramatizing his situation is to reveal him at point after point as already imprisoned by values to which he has been exposed. But in order to discover precisely what *The Pyramid* accomplishes, we must examine it more closely: first, its narrative structure; then some of the figures who people this world and Golding's characterization in the novel; finally, his meaning.

The Pyramid comprises three sections, each of them dwelling largely on the relationship between a younger Oliver and some other person in Stilbourne, the English village in which he has grown up before succeeding as a chemist. The first part describes the course of his involvement at the age of eighteen with Evie Babbacombe, the Town Crier's daughter, who ranks low in the social hierarchy so carefully preserved by Stilbourne but excites "every male for miles round."[1] The second section takes place several months later, on Oliver's return after his first term at Oxford, and records his encounter with Evelyn De Tracy, an outsider who has come to direct a production of the Stilbourne Operatic Society. In the third portion a middle-aged Oliver is drawn back to Stilbourne once more, where he learns of the death of Bounce Dawlish, relives several segments of his childhood when she was his music teacher, suddenly realizes as an adult what his feelings as a child about her were, then finally catches sight of the person he has become. Each section, while revealing a good deal about Stilbourne and Oliver's parents, themselves firmly imbedded in the life of the village, takes its governing shape from the progress of Oliver's acquaintance with another person to a significant event which ought to engender insight and sympathy in him. But in the first two events Oliver fails to comprehend the evidence before his eyes—in part an expression, I take it, of the degree to which his imagination is bound by the norms of Stilbourne—and, if he is temporarily moved by the third event, it does not essentially alter his response to the person in question. Although from time to time he reacts against Stilbourne's values, speaks as a social critic, or seems on the verge of breaking out from the self constituted by his family and society to engage immediately with another human, the trajectory of the novel as a whole shows Oliver arriving only at a perception of his inadequacy—in spite of the good will he so frequently displays and his normality, in spite of his successful career and the presumably happy marriage that we glimpse near the end of the story.

Although *The Pyramid* begins with a quickly paced adolescent escapade, the narrative movement through the opening of the novel's first section is rather leisurely as Golding, while detailing Oliver's fumbling attempts to win Evie for his pleasure, also sketches in the inhabitants of the village and its ways: the kindly father and waspish mother, thoroughly conventional, to both of whom Oliver is deeply attached; the Ewans next door, felt by all to be superior because the father is a doctor, a fact which young Bobby never forgets; Henry Williams, the friendly garageman (whom we shall see more of in the book's final section), and Captain Wilmot, wounded in the First World War and pensioned, who lives opposite Evie's family down in Chandler's Close and seems suspiciously fond of her; Sergeant Babbacombe, the violent father whose punishments Evie fears, and Mrs. Babbacombe, a joke to the village because she persists in greeting those above her—an utterly stratified society, in short, so fixed in its attitudes and intent upon all which goes in Stilbourne that Oliver, the son of a dispenser of medicines, cannot bring himself to walk along the main street with Evie. Oliver's pursuit of Evie itself is often treated comically by Golding through these opening pages, as in the episode at the start of the book where Oliver, inveigled by Evie, helps her current boyfriend, Bobby Ewan, rescue a borrowed car from a pond at midnight and return it to the village so that Evie may not be found out, or in the later scene of the fight between the rivals, where Bobby, who rather ridiculously feels insulted, dances scientifically about, only to be thrashed by an awkward Oliver as surprised by his victory as is Bobby. This initially comic effect, however, owes most to the reflections of Oliver himself, our point of view in the story: his extravagant reactions, heated imaginings of Evie, absurd plottings to secure her, and sense of guilt in lusting after her establish him as typically adolescent. But the tone darkens somewhat as social and familial pressures begin to mount along with Oliver's desire for Evie: because she lives in Chandler's Close, Oliver needs continually to avoid being seen with her; as Oliver discovers, Evie herself has masked her adventures with Bobby Ewan by pretending to her family that Oliver is really courting her, for they can just conceive of her gaining Oliver as a husband but not aspiring to Bobby; and Oliver must constantly cope with his attentive parents, who at one point forbid him to buy the damaged motor bike on which Bobby has taken Evie riding (in part, because Oliver's mother intuits his interest in Evie), whereupon the frustrated Oliver smashes his fist into the piano which his parents treasure primarily because he plays it. In the pages that follow, the narrative tempo itself speeds up through the series of sexual engagements between Oliver and Evie which are crucial to our understanding of *The Pyramid*'s first section.

In the prelude to Oliver's initial possession of Evie, he is so gripped by a combination of anger at Bobby's past successes with her, mortification at having broken the piano, and sheer physical need that he grabs her and tows her up a hill into a clump of trees, paying no attention to what she says. Evie does in fact cooperate, though at first with a "grin that was at once knowing and avid and contemptuous" (p. 55), and Oliver's immediate reaction to their designedly incomplete love-making is of his own physical relief. Then "Triumph and delight began to burgeon and spread in me," and, when Evie accuses him of regarding her merely as a sexual object, he toys with her possessively, apparently incapable of imagining her as anything else, and keeps relishing the egotistical thought that "I had *had* this sulky, feminine, gorgeous creature" after she returns to the village (pp. 56–57). On their second meeting in the clump of trees Evie, suddenly excited by the appearance of her father in the village below, begs the naïve Oliver to "*Hurt* me" while making love, but then retreats into a sexual world of her own in which "a partner was necessary but not welcome," and the spent Oliver quickly moves away from her to lie "with my face in the dead leaves" (pp. 62–63). As a result of this undesignedly completed experience, however, each of them starts blaming the other for Evie's possible pregnancy, apprehensive of its social consequences. After Evie utters her hatred for the town, Oliver is momentarily stirred to sympathize with her plight as a girl and say, "Cheer up. It may never happen," at which Evie "gave a kind of sob" (p. 64), a fact that conveys to Oliver her anxiety alone, though the reader may sense in it a feeling on her part that she has been rejected as a person in a new way by Oliver's words. In any case, during the next days Oliver can only brood on the impossibility of going on to Oxford if he has fathered a baby, or the sniggers that would be provoked if he were to pay maintenance for an illegitimate child, or the essential horror of marrying Evie because "it would kill" his parents "To be related, even if only by marriage, to *Sergeant Babbacombe*" (p. 65). But after a time he learns from Evie that they are safe and learns also (in a scene that I shall come back to later) that she has been beaten—by Captain Wilmot, as Oliver thinks—in a perverse sexual exercise. Oliver uses the knowledge to pressure her into new meetings—he regards her now as "my slave" (p. 73), a phrase that duplicates Bobby Ewan's earlier words to Oliver which have made friendship between those two impossible—but Evie counters by offering herself to him only out at the edge of the escarpment, in plain sight of the town, requiring at least this public acknowledgment from him. Oliver, though fearing "the eyes of Stilbourne on my back," is mastered by his desire, so takes her once more in an act marked by their alienation from each other: "She neither resisted nor co-operated; and afterwards, when I was gasping face downwards, she went away flushed, silent and ashamed" (p. 79). And they are indeed seen by Oliver's father, who has been peering through his binoculars at the escarpment because of a re-mark made to him earlier by Evie about the bestiality of all men, and whose parental reaction of muted shock confirms Oliver in his feelings of utter shame.

These three scenes are carefully framed to keep the reader conscious of Stilbourne and its pressures in the immediate background, pressures that always impinge upon and ulti-mately enclose the meetings of Evie and Oliver. His violence in the first one derives from his physical need, but also from his contempt for himself at pursuing Evie to satisfy that need, as well as from his guilt at just having struck the piano, a deed of brief rebellion against his parents; in the passage following the meeting, Oliver apologizes to his parents for the piano and overtly reconciles himself with them again. The second encounter is quite literally framed by two references to Evie's father in the village below, a man who may stir Evie in one way but who is for Oliver simply a part of that world in which "the depth of my offence was to be measured" (p. 64). And their final engagement, out in the open, is bounded on the one side by what Oliver thinks "an irrational fear" of being seen from Stilbourne "that laid a hand on my flesh, but a real one," and on the other by his sight of an "odd figure that moved here or there" down by his home, the father who in fact has observed him (p. 79). Informed as they are by the various pressures of Stilbourne, these meetings between Oliver and Evie—far from representing any experience of love that they share—chart their increasing separation from each other. The fundamental incapacity here, as I read *The Pyramid,* is Oliver's. Not that Evie is a lower-class angel in disguise, for she exhibits both malice and perversity; but Oliver is so conditioned by his world that he can hardly conceive of Evie as a person in her own right— and that he quite misconstrues the evidence of her real situation when it is revealed to him.

The misunderstood revelation occurs shortly after Evie has told Oliver that she is not pregnant, "mimicked . . . savagely" his "Thank God," and declared, "That's all you want, just my damned body, not me," to all of which Oliver responds in a kind of parody of mutual involvement, "wanting her to share" his delicious sense of "joy and freedom" (p. 70). Although recognizing that "She wanted tenderness" and "So did I; but not from her" (p. 71), Oliver starts after what he does want from her by flicking up her skirt, only to find her body covered with welts. He immediately believes Captain Wilmot to be responsible—despite the association of Sergeant Babbacombe with beating earlier in the story, Evie's constantly heightened reaction to the naming of her father, or her manifest sexual excitement on hearing his voice just before she begs Oliver to "Take me" and *"Hurt* me" at their second meeting on the hill—presumably because nothing during Oliver's life in Stilbourne has prepared him to imag-

ine a depraved relationship between father and daughter.
Even given his misinterpretation, Oliver can only utter "a
laugh of sheer incredulity" initially. Then, although Evie
blushes, thus acknowledging the normal response to the situation that she supposes Oliver to see clearly, yet also half
defends that situation in saying "I was sorry for 'im," Oliver
reacts by further detaching himself, first looking down at his
parents in their garden, then back at Evie, "this object, on
an earth that smelt of decay . . . life's lavatory" (pp. 72–73).
When she offers to buy his silence by doing "Anything you
want" (p. 73), however, Oliver is ready enough to exploit
his power over her.

What I have just said no doubt makes Oliver himself
appear too villainous, whereas the novel merely represents
him as the prisoner of attitudes imbibed through growing up
in Stilbourne. They determine his insensitive treatment of
Evie—still apparent when he meets her for the last time, in a
coda to the first section of *The Pyramid,* some two years after
their affair has ended and Evie been eased out of Stilbourne
—and they undermine the glimpse he finally catches of the
relationship he might have had with her. At first, while the
two drink together in the Crown at Stilbourne, Oliver regards Evie as he always has: sexually exciting—"this evening
might be led," he speculates—and socially inferior—to her
claim about looking up some people in Stilbourne Oliver
replies, "You? What people?" (p. 87). He even mentions
Captain Wilmot without a qualm, as if no one like Evie
could resent the intended innuendo. But she caps all his
leading remarks by announcing to those present that Oliver
has raped her two years earlier; and, though she soon apologizes, she also berates him for his sense of social superiority
and consequent ignorance, as well as accuses him of "telling"
the whole town "an' laughing" about "Me 'n Dad" before

she walks away. Not really understanding her accusation, Oliver is nevertheless startled by her criticism into almost escaping his social preconceptions and seeing her clearly: "It was as if this object of frustration and desire had suddenly acquired the attributes of a person rather than a thing; as if I might—as if *we* might—have made something, music, perhaps, to take the place of the necessary, the inevitable battle" (p. 90). But Oliver, although "tempted for a moment to follow her," sees a light come on in his parents' house and so goes home "to brood on this undiscovered person and her curious slip of the tongue [in mentioning her father rather than Captain Wilmot]" (p. 91), his last phrase indicating how imperceptive Oliver remains despite his temporarily altered view of Evie.

The second section of *The Pyramid* contains no graded sequence like the meetings between Evie and Oliver, but it does advance, as did the initial movement, toward the revelation of another person in a reasonably extreme human situation, a revelation which Oliver again fails to comprehend. Returning to the village after his first term at Oxford and worrying a bit about seeing Imogen once more (an older girl, now married, whom he has idealized), Oliver finds a production of the Stilbourne Operatic Society in full swing and is soon badgered by his proud mother into taking a bit part as a violin player. The opening half of the section demonstrates how completely the production is governed by Stilbourne's social sense, while the rehearsal that we witness also exhibits a number of personal jealousies as Oliver's mother schemes to make the most of her son's role or quarrels with Imogen's husband, himself a ridiculously arrogant figure, over the military title by which Oliver should be addressed in the performance. Through all these pages, the life of Stilbourne is represented by details more exaggerated than those of the first section; the characters are more thinly drawn; and the comic effects are prevailingly bitter. The character in the foreground here is less Oliver than Evelyn De Tracy, a professional in the theater who comes to the village intent only on his fee of "Ten guineas and a third-class return" (p. 120), views Stilbourne with a contempt manifest in the scarcely concealed laughter that constantly shakes him, and successfully manipulates everyone with excessive flattery. In the course of the actual performance, he repairs to the Crown for drinks with Oliver, where De Tracy refers to Stilbourne's shortcomings and also begins to free Oliver from his "calf-love" for Imogen through analyzing accurately her vanity (p. 121), yet De Tracy is really interested in thus curing Oliver to win the young man for himself. When Oliver, liberated by his drink, momentarily breaks through the "walls" of his life to speak as a critic of Stilbourne himself ("the way we hide our bodies and the things we don't say . . . the people we don't meet"), to tell Evelyn of the affair with an Evie now almost regarded as a person ("she was just a country girl from Chandler's Close; though come to think of it, why on earth we—"), and to declare, "I want the *truth* of things. But there's nowhere to find it" (pp. 122–23), the hopeful producer hands him photographs of De Tracy dressed up as a girl in a "ballerina's costume" (p. 124). But the sheltered Oliver proves even less capable of understanding this evidence than Evie's welts, and again he responds with laughter. Although he is indeed freed by De Tracy to see Imogen as she is and although he befriends the drunken producer by helping him get out of town, Oliver's essential alignment with the world of Stilbourne is suggested by his incomprehension of De Tracy. Golding reinforces the suggestion, I think, by placing those talks with De Tracy in which Oliver's horizon expands some-

what between the scene of his public triumph at the performance—when, applauded on his appearance because he is
"the dispenser's son . . . one of the right sort of people" (p.
118), Oliver forgets every instruction in displaying his musical virtuosity, much to the delight of his mother—and the
closing paragraph of the second section, in which he returns,
after putting De Tracy on a bus, "to receive my congratulations" at a party backstage (p. 130).

The final section of *The Pyramid* is slightly more complicated in structure, the visit of an adult Oliver to Stilbourne
and his ultimate assessment of his life framing a group of
remembered experiences with Bounce Dawlish, his former
music teacher. Generally speaking, those remembrances are
shaped so as, first, to make progressively clearer to the reader
the exploitation of the unattractive Miss Dawlish by a Henry
Williams winning in manner yet intent upon succeeding in
business, and second, to develop a subdued tension between
the social formula which Oliver accepts as describing his
own relationship to his teacher—"He's *devoted* to Miss Dawlish—aren't you, dear?" (p. 143) —and the actual mixture of
fear, superiority, and pity that he feels.

Bounce Dawlish is the daughter of a "failed" artist, a man
who has turned himself "into the portrait of a romantic
musician" and so gives "Stilbourne a painless excuse to feel
that it was in touch with the arts"—especially since he possesses some property and a little money (pp. 136–37). Thus
her father and her profession as teacher confer a certain
status on Miss Dawlish, though it becomes apparent that she
is ill-fitted for her job and has been ruthlessly bullied by her
father into taking up music. Heavyset, homely, mannishly
dressed, she seems a typically forbidding teacher until the
affable Henry Williams turns up in Stilbourne. Full of good
will though he is, Henry yet plays upon her growing affec

tion for him to sell her a car, settle in Stilbourne on the death of her father, establish himself in business at her expense, move into her house with his "quite unforeseen wife and child" (p. 155), then move out—after making so much noise in his work that Bounce can hardly hold her lessons—to take over her father's cottage and "build a garage" (p. 160). Henry's exploitation of her is punctuated by many indications of Bounce's frustrated love: her sudden appearance dressed as a woman and made up at one of Oliver's lessons, when she reads the "incredulity" in his eyes (p. 154); the "ludicrously pleading" words that he later overhears, "All I want is for you to need me, need me!" (p. 158); or the picture he sketches of her, on the night Henry leaves the house, down on her knees before the fire, "trying to learn unsuccessfully, without a teacher, how to sob her heart out" (p. 168). The village itself, of course, views the entire affair with a mixture of distrust for Henry, contempt for Bounce's weakness in letting herself be used, and triumph at her misery: the arrival of Henry's "unforeseen" family, for example, proves "a most exhilarating time for everyone" (p. 155). In the third section of *The Pyramid*, Golding portrays Stilbourne as inveterately curious about its inhabitants and less than sympathetically disposed towards them, attitudes which Oliver himself reflects in some of his encounters with Bounce Dawlish. When her pursuit of Henry takes about the only form it still can—a series of deliberate car accidents which enable her to call him for help—Oliver's mother explains to him Bounce's actions, a standing joke in the town; and for a moment this enlightenment consumes him "with humiliation, resentment and a sort of stage fright, to think how we were all known, all food for each other," but shortly he can wonder, "amused and cynical" as the rest, what Bounce's "next step" may be (pp. 173–74).

Oliver's own relations with her seem always strained, partly because, as a child, he often misses the full significance of her odd behavior, sometimes keeping details of it to himself, and partly because society's dictum that he is "devoted" to her inhibits his recognition of his true response. Oliver is also trapped by his world in another way through this closing movement of *The Pyramid,* which shows him yearning for a musical career, yet acceding to his parents' ideal of success, the "scholarship at Oxford" and study of "Physics and Chemistry"—"the real, the serious thing"—which will make the "world" his "oyster" (p. 162). Bounce need merely mention Oliver's mother and father for him to realize "the *obscenity* of erratic, unpensioned music," and the eccentric teacher echoes for once the sentiments of society, though bitterly commenting on her own situation, in remarking, "Don't be a musician. . . . Go into the garage business if you want to make money. As for me, I shall have to slave at music till I drop down dead" (pp. 162–63). While Oliver fulfills all too well society's ideal in his ensuing success as a chemist, he also makes several discoveries about himself and Bounce which might promise to stir an acute personal sympathy in him for her, but leave him finally rather helplessly enclosed in the self he has become. The climactic step in her efforts to claim Henry's attention is to present herself on the street wearing hat, gloves, shoes, and "nothing else whatsoever"; although Oliver feels "a storm" within him at this revelation of her need—there's no question of his laughing here as he has at Evie's welts or the photographs of De Tracy —he instinctively tries to repress the sight ("No. No. Oh-No") even as he knows that it "was seared into me . . . ineradicable" (p. 175). Later, after having reviewed his past with her while sitting as an adult at Bounce's grave, he suddenly bursts out in "wanton laughter" at the realization that he has always hated her. But ironically even this seized truth—of the dislike for her which society has conditioned him to repress—cannot be fully assimilated by Oliver, who first runs away from the realization, then can articulate it precisely to himself—*"I was afraid of you, and so I hated you. . . . When I heard you were dead I was glad"*—only when safely enveloped within a sense of "the security of my own warm life" in the conventional world (p. 180). Although he goes back to Bounce's house once more, he cannot exorcise the fear he has known as a child for her, and although he discovers—in the burned music and destroyed photographs at the end of her garden—proof of her continuing victimization by her father and ultimate rebellion against him, Oliver still cannot break out of himself into a thoroughly compassionate response: "I did not know to what or whom my feelings had reference, nor even what they were" (p. 182). If he thinks briefly, in the closing paragraphs of *The Pyramid,* of telling Henry that Bounce was her truest self—"calm and happy" for "the only time"— when she walked naked to Henry's garage, only to be "put . . . away" by Stilbourne "until she was properly cured and unhappy again," Oliver in fact remains silent, for "really, you could say nothing" (p. 182). And though he momentarily wishes for the chance to reshape his life, he realizes how firmly he is trapped within a being molded by society: looking at Henry, the well-disposed man who is yet committed to worldly success, Oliver sees at last "my own face" (p. 183).

The minor characters of *The Pyramid,* as well as some of the major ones, not only serve to flesh out the stratified world in which Oliver grows up but stand as instances themselves of Stilbourne's pervasive social consciousness. At the top of the scale are Imogen Claymore and her husband, owner of the local paper; awareness of their position combines with their personal vanity to assure them that Stilbourne owes them homage: he cannot even mention his part in a pageant without exhibiting his superiority. "I had a sword, a horse and a whole troop of servants!" (p. 107), and Imogen is properly outraged when Oliver's awkward entrance with a halberd forces her husband to bend down on the stage. The family of Dr. Ewan also ranks high, with the result that Bobby continually patronizes the dispenser's son and responds to a ridiculously irrelevant insult by Oliver as if it were a serious challenge to his honor by an inferior. Old Mr. Dawlish has forced Bounce's career of music teacher on her as one way of acting out his role as Stilbourne's artist. In the lower reaches of the scale, social differentiation still obtains: Mrs. Babbacombe may be looked down upon by much of Stilbourne as "about our only Roman Catholic" and a greeter of those above her, but she herself will "not mix with the riffraff of Chandlers' Close" (p. 31), the section of town in which she lives. Henry Williams is regarded with suspicion and resentment during his first months in Stilbourne because he is an outsider, a nobody trying to establish himself in the garage business through using Bounce Dawlish. Although he often behaves with real good will and affection, as in helping Oliver conceal his interest in Evie or in treating Bounce herself as a "dear, kind lady" (p. 156), the novel represents Henry as above all a man who capitalizes upon his accommodating manner to get on, whether in mediating between his quarrelsome wife and the jealous Bounce while they all live together or in achieving—at Bounce's expense —his ultimate status as Stilbourne's leading businessman. He reveals his social awareness in the arrangement itself of the motto which he has had inscribed on Bounce's tomb, the "three words in small lettering" near "the foot" of the memorial which convey to the adult Oliver Henry's "modest assurance, his sense of position, of who was entitled to do what" (p. 136). And Henry's fundamental commitment to a sort of success valued by the world is openly formulated by Oliver at one point, when he interprets the fact that Henry is impressed by an expensive car and by the implied prestige as marking an "attitude . . . typical of the deep thing lying in him, the reason for it all, tarmac, glass, concrete, machinery, the thrust not liked or enjoyed but recognized as inevitable, the god without mercy" (p. 133).

Oliver's parents are felt fairly continually by the reader as presences in *The Pyramid,* transmitting Stilbourne's attitudes to their son while they love him so genuinely and plan so attentively for his future that the occasions on which he resists them fill him with guilt—when in their affection they propose to have rebuilt the piano Oliver has smashed, for instance, he weeps in gratitude and shame. The father is an eminently kindly man, ready to think the best of everyone (he even defends Henry Williams against the attacks of Oliver's mother), yet so oriented to conventional ideas of success that he instinctively imagines "the profession of music," to which his son is naturally inclined, as "perilous" and necessarily involving Oliver's descent "through a course of indescribable bohemianism" to poverty (p. 138). In the one episode where the father is less than kind, driven by Evie's talk of man's bestiality to spy through his binoculars on his son (spying is an activity recurrently linked with society in the book), Oliver's father reproaches him by invoking the specter of venereal disease traditionally associated with a lower-class girl and then by speaking, "for all his professed but indifferent agnosticism," with "the voice of generations of chapel": ". . . these books—cinema—papers —this sex—it's *wrong, wrong, wrong!*" (p. 81)—a reproach which Oliver takes firmly to himself in thinking, when he next sees Evie, "She was wrong, wrong, wrong; and so was I" (p. 82). Oliver's mother is as nasty as his father is kindly. She intuits every threat to the person she wants Oliver to become, so violently dislikes Evie, responding to Bobby Ewan's injury on a motorcycle with "Nobody else was hurt —more's the pity!" (p. 44). She reveals her foolishness and pettiness by admiring the light opera performed at Stilbourne, by bending every effort to put her son forward in the performance, and by preening herself on De Tracy's gross flattery at the same time that she scornfully notes it as De Tracy's means of manipulating the Claymores. Indeed, she epitomizes Stilbourne: resenting Henry Williams; maintaining that Oliver is "devoted" to his music teacher, even though the mother wonders with malicious delight—after another accident by which Bounce has contrived to meet Henry—what the frustrated woman will "do when she runs out of 'phone boxes" (p. 173) ; or spying at every chance on the other inhabitants of the village.

As I have already suggested in outlining the structure of *The Pyramid*, three characters in effect offer Oliver the opportunity to break through the attitudes ingrained in him into loving, or at least sympathizing with, another, and each of the three functions to some extent as a critic of Stilbourne. De Tracy is by all odds the thinnest of these figures, little more than a caricature of the sophisticated city dweller. Although he may guide Oliver towards a true estimate of Imogen, his motive is to secure the young man for himself. If his scarcely suppressed laughter at nearly everything that happens indicates his insight into and contempt of the village, he yet hypocritically flatters everyone, ready enough to live off the world that he despises.

Evie's reactions to life in Stilbourne are more variously

detailed than De Tracy's, and she strikes me as a much more complex character—despite what seem important obscurities in Golding's presentation of her, obscurities that perhaps owe something to the limitations of Oliver's insight. Her banal wishes for the future typify the longings of a lower-class girl who feels trapped in a small town: "Oh I should like to fly more than anything! And . . . to dance—and sing, of course—and travel—I should like to do everything!" (p. 41). As we have seen, she frequently reproaches Oliver for his upper-class treatment of her as a sexual object instead of as a person in her own right (Golding endows her with a musical talent and a desire to learn, if only typing, both of which imply that Oliver might properly value her in ways other than he does). And she accurately though somewhat inarticulately criticizes Oliver as well as Stilbourne at their final encounter: "*You!* Aren't you ever going to grow up? This place—you. You an' your mum and dad. Too good for people, aren't you? You got a bathroom. 'I'm going to Oxford!' You don' know about—cockroaches an'—well" (p. 90). Although Evie's sense of Stilbourne itself is clear enough, some of her motives and feelings appear to me obscure. Why has she talked about the bestiality of men to Oliver's father in such a way as to arouse his suspicions: unintentionally, because she is dominated by her experience with her father? or intentionally, because she wants revenge against an Oliver who has previously been overjoyed to find that she is not pregnant? What does she really feel for her father: the hatred suggested by her generalizations about men? or the sympathy explicit in "I was sorry for 'im" (p. 72)? or the dark pleasure implicit in the "sneering grin" with which she sometimes greets Oliver's advances (p. 55) and in the "faint smile" with which she recalls being beaten at fifteen, "as if she were remembering something shymaking

but good" (p. 73) ? or a combination of the three? Does she
know that Stilbourne has expelled her because a trace of her
lipstick has been observed on the face of Dr. Ewan's assist-
ant? or does she think—quite wrongly—that the reason is
Oliver's disclosure of her relationship with her father? And
why, when she publicly accuses Oliver of having raped her,
does she claim to have been "only just fifteen" (p. 89) : is she
simply trying to blacken Oliver further? or is she enacting a
private compulsion to clear her father, at least in her own
eyes, by linking Oliver with her decisive experience at fifteen? Although Evie's response to what has happened between her father and herself thus remains to some degree
puzzlingly equivocal, her behavior at many moments reveals
an integrated complexity. While she prefers Bobby Ewan to
Oliver—relishing her escapades with the doctor's son, blaming herself for his injury on a motorcycle, and praying for his
recovery—she is yet physically attracted by Oliver, certainly
desirous of entering into a personal relationship with him,
and perhaps hopeful of finally winning him. Many of these
strands of feeling are caught together in her response when
Oliver first pulls her up the hill to the clump of trees: relief
at the news she has just heard that Bobby is not seriously
injured; an excitement responsive to Oliver's urgent need of
her body; the drive to advance her own claims as an individual, "What I'm trying to say is, everything's different—see—
if you could only—" (p. 55) —though Oliver does not even
listen to the rest of her words. Similarly complex is Evie's
motivation when she later compels Oliver to take her, if he
will, in plain sight on the escarpment. Her action represents
simultaneously her own pressure in kind exerted against
Oliver, who willingly uses his knowledge of Evie's welts to
force her to meet him; her sense that the upper-class Oliver is
hardly likely thus to expose himself; her bitter determina-

tion that, if he should take her, he make at least this public acknowledgment of her; and her general defiance of Stilbourne.

Bounce Dawlish is a comparably detailed character who develops into more than a stereotype of a Stilbourne eccentric just as Evie develops into more than a stereotype of the town's loose woman. Bullied by Mr. Dawlish into a career for which she has no talent, Bounce may frighten her students and amuse the spiteful village by her pathetic efforts to attach Henry Williams, but she also compels our sympathy. Attracted by Henry, she can rebel against her father to the extent of buying a car, but she remains haunted by her fear of Mr. Dawlish even after his death, crying out with terror when she once discovers Oliver in the darkened music room presided over by the photograph of her father; and much later she shows a real similarity to her father in protesting against Oliver's listening to records by musical masters—"I would never, *never* listen to anything so cheap, nasty, vulgar, blasphemous—" (p. 156) —the passage harking back to an incident in which Mr. Dawlish has smashed a phonograph. To the family which Henry has moved into her home she responds with a mixture of possessiveness and bitterness. An expression of her frustrated love for Henry himself, long after he has moved out to set up his own household and expand his business, is shot through with emotional complexity:

> "He always services my car himself—changes the oil and all those things, things inside, I don't know what they are. And he always cleans it himself, washes it, polishes it. He puts on overalls and gets down to it just like he—" (p. 170)

Her words carry a suggestion of upper-class disdain for sheerly mechanical knowledge and a trace of pride as she describes the exertions of a social inferior. But it is clear that in the main she cherishes Henry's care, interpreting it as the demonstration he allows himself of his affection for her. The last, uncompleted sentence precisely dramatizes an appropriate muddle of feelings in her: gratification that he should love or revere the car because it is a surrogate for her, as well as contempt that he should lavish such attentions on a mere automobile. Against the background of Stilbourne itself Bounce does indeed stand forth as an eccentric, compelled by her love for Henry to appear as her naked self, frightening, unattractive, pathetic. Unlike Evie and De Tracy, she does not achieve any real accommodation with the world. When Oliver last sees her, the house filled with birds and cats, she interrupts his hypocritically conventional attempt to "thank" her for all her lessons with "Don't bother. It doesn't mean anything, does it," then goes on to tell him, "Do you know . . . ? If I could save a child or a budgie from a burning house, I'd save the budgie" (p. 179). And her final commentary on life in Stilbourne is her destruction, before dying, of her father's photograph and of the music by which she has supported herself in the village.

In discussing the structure and characters, I have been maintaining that Stilbourne itself is the central power in *The Pyramid,* influencing all its inhabitants after some fashion and often shaping Oliver more thoroughly than he realizes. One indication of its dominance over him is that Oliver frequently returns to the town imagining himself somehow changed, yet rapidly sinking back into the ways of Stilbourne again. I use the word "indication" rather than "symbol" or some such term because the verbal mode in this novel almost never encourages the reader—through some use of language manifestly charged in one way or another—to sense that any particular detail is fraught with special significance: Golding's mode here—so prevailingly realistic that there seems no point in analyzing a sample of the prose—is tailored, I take it, to the essential imperceptiveness of his narrator, who for the most part re-creates rather literalistically a world out there, as it were, and reports objectively on the behavior of his more youthful self in it. Certainly Golding pursues his theme by showing his narrator so impregnated with or immediately responsive to the values of Stilbourne as to suggest that, for someone like Oliver, at least, the pressures of environment are inescapable.

Thus Oliver always considers his desire for Evie, as would the town, a proof of his wickedness. Or he understands "as by nature" why "the son of Dr. Ewan couldn't take the daughter of Sergeant Babbacombe to a dance in his father's car" (p. 9). Bobby Ewan's comically triumphant description of his posture in making love to Evie is exactly the sort of account that the doctor's son naturally gives and Oliver receives without demur because Evie is their social inferior. Amusingly enough, when Bobby will not answer his rival's greeting after their fight, Oliver does not laugh at the ridiculous figure that Bobby cuts but feels "humiliated and ashamed," so deep-seated is his conviction of Bobby's superior station. Oliver's family is for him so inextricably rooted in Stilbourne society that the two operate on him almost as one force. His marriage to Evie, he feels, "would kill" his parents: "To be related, even if only by marriage, to *Sergeant Babbacombe!* I saw their social world, so delicately poised and carefully maintained, so fiercely defended, crash into the gutter" (p. 65). And later, on the escarpment with

Evie, Oliver "felt the eyes of Stilbourne on my back; but they were distant, they wore pebble glasses, and we were two inscrutable specks" (p. 79)—the "pebble glasses" always worn by Oliver's father here identifying him with the village itself in Oliver's emotions. Even as a child Oliver is sufficiently aware of his status to refuse a tip for delivering medicine, "I knew I was not a Poor Boy" (p. 149). If he quite unwittingly betrays to Bounce Dawlish society's judgment of her in saying that Henry is "using a sprat to catch a mackerel," the young Oliver simply "delighted" at employing "a new phrase" (p. 151), his response of "incredulity" to her appearance in feminine attire at one of the lessons exhibits precisely the reaction to be expected from Stilbourne at large. Indeed, the influence of the town on Oliver is never eradicated: during his final return to the village as a success, he is "conscious of impressing" Henry and walks about "accepting this deference" even though "contemptuous of the way in which our social antennae had vibrated" (p. 133).

Although most of the instances just cited show an Oliver unaware of Stilbourne's grip on his being, he is moved periodically towards a more objective view of the town that can sometimes enable him to criticize it—but in each case Stilbourne retains its hold on him. After seeing Evie's welts and then looking down at his parents in the village, Oliver discovers in himself "a tremendous feeling of thereness and hereness, of separate worlds, they and Imogen, clean in that coloured picture; here, this object, on an earth that smelt of decay, with picked bones and natural cruelty—life's lavatory" (p. 73), and the very colors of his words make clear that it is the Stilbourne world with which Oliver links himself instinctively. Helped on by a drink, he may complain to De Tracy that "Everything's—*wrong*. . . . There's no truth and there's no honesty. My God! Life can't—I mean just out there, you have only to look up at the sky—but Stilbourne accepts it as a *roof*" (p. 122), yet Oliver proves as unable as the rest of the town to see De Tracy for the man he is. If he decides in a corner of his family's garden—"where I was not only away from people, but as nearly as possible away from the pressure of them"—to pursue a musical career, Bounce has only to speak of his parents for Oliver to feel the *"obscenity"* of his desire and abandon it (p. 162). He even comes, we may remember, to regard Bounce's accidents with the town's mixture of amusement and cynicism, although on first learning of her motives from his parents Oliver has been "consumed with humiliation, resentment and a sort of stage fright, to think how we were all known, all food for each other, all clothed and ashamed in our clothing" (p. 173) — significantly, Golding here allies the Fall of Man and its tonalities with the functioning of a social organism rather than with an exercise of will by the individual.

Late in the novel, confronted with the pathetic wreck of womanhood in Bounce Dawlish, Oliver tells us of his "fierce determination" that his own daughter shall "never know such lost solemnity but be a fulfilled woman, a wife and mother" (p. 179), yet in fact we never see enough of his family to make any informed guess about how his children may develop. The evidence on Oliver himself, however, is unambiguous: freedom for him from the influences of society is, practically speaking, a hypothesis and no more. His voice—even when he is surprised into declaring the reality of his unacknowledged dislike for Bounce while standing alone at her tomb—can only cry out "as if it could make its own bid for honesty," and Oliver quickly suppresses the realization as his social self reasserts its mastery (p. 180). On the last page of the novel, he may perceive how Stilburne has enclosed his own life:

I stood, looking down at the worn pavement, so minutely and illegibly inscribed; and I saw the feet, my own among them, pass and repass. I stretched out a leg and tapped with my live toe . . . and suddenly I felt that if I might only lend my own sound, my own flesh, my own power of choosing the future, to those invisible feet, I would pay anything—*anything*: but knew in the same instant that, like Henry, I would never pay more than a reasonable price. (pp. 182–83)

But he also recognizes that, even if he could somehow purchase the freedom to re-form the life that Stilbourne has shaped, he would make no sacrifice for that freedom, so dominated is he by the attitudes of the man he has become.

It may seem fanciful to describe the Oliver represented in *The Pyramid* as stillborn, incapable of emerging into a substantially personal life because his self is so thoroughly constituted by his parents and the surrounding world. Yet surely the name of the village functions in part as a pun to suggest the essential deadness of life in Stilbourne and the stultifying effect of the town's conventions on its inhabitants. Similarly, although the only specific mention in the novel of a pyramid—Oliver remembers "how the Ewans," more highly placed than his own family, "always gave me a present at Christmas. They also vibrated in time to the crystal pyramid" (p. 150)—allies it with a social structure that narrows sharply from base to apex, the pyramid embodied in the world of Stilbourne also proves to be a tomb for Oliver. Perhaps even his narrative itself might be regarded as a pyramid of sorts in that Oliver re-creates for us a group of experiences which enshrine the past of a successful man yet reveal him as entombed within it. However that may be, *The Pyramid* is decidedly somber in depicting the power of the human environment to mold imperceptibly the values of the individual and in effect annihilate him. Yet it would be rash, I think, to interpret the book as an absolute statement by Golding about the helplessness of the individual in the face of society, for Oliver, though normal in many respects, is at times so radically imperceptive as to seem a special case. And his consciousness, both as a narrator of what has happened and as an adult who has succeeded in the world and made an apparently happy marriage, is not sufficiently detailed for us either to feel that we really know the whole Oliver, so can see him clearly as an Everyman, or to identify his plight with our own as human beings. But certainly in *The Pyramid* Golding has broken with the earlier novels in concerning himself with the social rather than moral pressures exerted on man. What this shift in theme may signify for Golding's future work, however, or what the realistic mode of *The Pyramid* may portend for his artistic development, only the novels to come can tell us for sure.

1. *The Pyramid* (New York, 1967), p. 7; this is the edition to which I shall give further page references in my text.

Conclusion

If the foregoing chapters have helped to clarify the arguments of William Golding's novels, they will have served a useful purpose, I feel; and even if I have misinterpreted certain events or read the essential meanings of the later novels wrongly, my errors themselves may help others to arrive at the truth. But I hope at least that the chapters have demonstrated the narrative power of Golding's books, the fundamental requirement, after all, that any story must fulfill. Thematically obscure as the novels may be, this power makes itself felt—even when the reader does not immediately grasp the full significance of every detail—in those carefully graduated series of incidents which might be said to constitute the signature of all Golding's narratives up to *The Pyramid*. These incidents are what generate the initial impact of his fiction on every reader, and, such is Golding's strength as a storyteller, I think they retain their primary efficacy as narrative happenings despite the weight of meaning that they come to bear—although some critics have contended that Golding too obviously controls his narrative to fit the significance of the fable which he imagines. While the endings of the earlier books may indeed fracture, distressingly for some readers, the illusion of actuality nourished by the stories that have gone before, this fact is itself a testimony to the force of Golding's narratives. But, as I have already suggested, the objection to these endings on the ground of realism seems to me critically naïve; in any case, they function compellingly in their different ways to bring the issues of the novels home to the reader.

A deficiency with which Golding may more legitimately be charged, in my opinion, is his relative weakness as a creator of characters, a weakness one becomes more conscious of when placing Golding's works against those by the major English novelists of the past. Although such central characters as Ralph and Piggy, Lok and Fa, Pincher Martin, Sammy Mountjoy, and Dean Jocelin reveal complex lives of their own, many of the lesser figures appear thin in comparison, their behavior determined too exclusively by their significance in relation to the leading characters or by the theme of the story in question. And until the appearance of *The Pyramid,* I would have maintained that Golding had failed to create a densely detailed and thoroughly convincing representation of a woman. Winningly human as Fa is, she can hardly qualify as such a figure, for we simply do not see enough of her; Mary Lovell, Beatrice Ifor, and Goody Pangall are all subdued as persons by operating as foils to the leading characters; perhaps Golding wished the Taffy of *Free Fall* to be such a full-blooded individual, but we really have only Sammy Mountjoy's word for her vitality. Both Evie and Bounce Dawlish in *The Pyramid,* however, seem to me more fully imagined and complexly motivated than Golding's female characters in the earlier books—though he has yet to sustain a portrait in depth of a woman through an entire novel.

To mention Golding in the same breath with the major novelists of English literature will no doubt appear presumptuous to many, an instance of my being carried away by enthusiasm for a contemporary. Yet his books, taken as a whole, seem to me to ally Golding rather with the more traditional novelists of the past than with the writers of the present. Although in *Free Fall* Sammy Mountjoy is an artist and an extremely self-conscious narrator, the story neither treats, through Sammy, the problem of the artist as a special kind of person nor becomes a novel whose subject in any significant way is the writing of a novel—both of them particularly prominent motifs in twentieth-century literature. As for the concept of the anti-novel, it strikes me as the very reverse of what Golding seeks to achieve through his carefully articulated plots and his orientation of all materials to express his theme. If in his novels Golding does not attempt to reproduce—for the purpose of faithfully mirroring the condition of ordinary existence—the sheer flow of experience as the external world impinges on the consciousness of an observer, neither does he develop through his stories an image of a neutral universe with which it is folly for the individual to interact, the sort of universe which Robbe-Grillet has contended that a novelist should aspire to record. While in the matter of technique Golding is both adventurous and highly resourceful—as in adjusting the point of view of *The Inheritors* to Lok's extraordinary sense perceptions, in interweaving different levels of awareness to reveal gradually the situation of Pincher Martin, in unifying the apparently dislocated fragments that make up Sammy Mountjoy's story, or in shifting his own style to a degree from book to book—still one could scarcely classify Golding's techniques themselves as radically experimental. Probably the most salient technical innovation in his earlier books is the change in focus at their conclusions, but the change testifies to the concern that Golding shares with more traditional novelists to convey his theme to the reader as forcefully as possible.

And when I think back to the established English novelists, I cannot help sensing important similarities between Golding's fiction and Thomas Hardy's. To be sure, Golding lacks Hardy's imaginative power in the creation of character. But both writers are acute observers of the natural world, rendering the settings of their novels so substantially that the physical world may become a living thing. Both are extremely gifted storytellers, with Golding's narratives often the more sparely presented and the more meticulously controlled, but Hardy's developing a similar momentum as they advance through a series of memorable scenes to an inescapable conclusion. Both novelists are possessed by their themes, relentlessly exploring the condition of man as they see it, however differently they evaluate that condition. And both of them leave one with an impression of singular honesty, for they hold fast to their essential visions of man and refuse to compromise with beliefs and attitudes more conventional at the time of their writing. Whether Golding's novels will endure as Hardy's have, only the future can tell, but the achievement of his fiction so far, as well as the nature of his themes and his seriousness in pursuing them, encourage one to judge his work by standards no lower than those set by the traditional English novel.

To speak of Golding's achievement in the body of his work is a good deal easier than to generalize effectively about his development to this point in time as a novelist, for *The Pyramid*—so unpredictable, I think, in the light of its predecessors—appears to break decisively in technique and theme with what has gone before. Whereas four of the first five novels are grounded in a sequence of events that accumulate an enormous narrative charge (and even *Free Fall* depends on such a sequence in the central episode of Sammy Mountjoy in the concentration camp), *The Pyramid* feels much more loosely structured, with only the three sexual encounters between Oliver and Evie in the first part of the story affecting one as a sequence that advances narratively with something like the thrust of those in the earlier books. In the earlier novels, as well, the subjective experience of main characters so various as the youthful Ralph or Dean Jocelin is richly imagined by Golding, and densely represented, too, in the case of Lok's sensuous apprehension of the world, or the existence which Pincher Martin has willed for himself, or the combination of remembered events with commentary through which Sammy Mountjoy re-creates his past; yet *The Pyramid* offers no such vital center in Oliver, whose inner life remains comparatively empty even while he tells us his story. Similarly, Golding's style itself in *The Pyramid* seems relaxed and colorless in comparison with the controlled symbolism in *Lord of the Flies*, the marvellous evocation of the world as sensed by a primitive in *The Inheritors*, the interlocking of the apparently substantial and the subjective in *Pincher Martin*, the rendition of a religious dimension in *Free Fall*, or the spare, taut verbal mode of *The Spire*. But, as I have already implied in discussing *The Pyramid*, all of its technical differences may be viewed as consequences of an attempt to represent a presumably rather ordinary person so deeply conditioned by society that he is hardly aware of the ways in which it smothers him—which may be to suggest, once more, that Golding typically creates his fictional structures in the service of meaning.

More striking than *The Pyramid*'s structural innovations, however, is its shift in theme from the previous novels. For they comprise a sustained investigation into the nature of man from a Christian perspective. If *Lord of the Flies* and *The Inheritors* treat social groups, Golding has nevertheless maintained that the "moral" of the first book—the same might be said of the second—"is that the shape of a society must depend on the ethical nature of the individual" [1]; and the religious overtones in each story, however muted, function to define "ethical" behavior for us. The next three novels isolate individuals involved in one fashion or another with religious experience, proceeding from Pincher Martin, who attempts to deny everything not fathered by his ego, through Sammy Mountjoy, who is capable of visions informed by divinity, to Dean Jocelin, who learns to acknowledge his guilty self and seeks to abandon it. Yet in all these books, as I have argued, Golding persists in representing even those who experience the divine as fundamentally limited by their humanity, and it is difficult to imagine—for me, at any rate—how the particular theme might be pursued in new ways beyond *The Spire.* In *The Pyramid,* where a religious perspective no longer operates significantly, Golding appears for the first time to conceive of society itself as man's decisive antagonist rather than the individual's fallen nature. But whether the novel indicates that Golding has now begun to view society as an entity absolutely hostile to, necessarily limiting the development of, the individual is hard to say because *The Pyramid* does not supply us with sufficient data on Oliver to make clear how responsible he may be as a person for what happens to him. Although how Golding may come to elaborate in the future on the relationship between the self and society is beyond guessing, there is a potentially allied subject—touched on in several of his stories so far—which one might wish that he will find occasion to explore: a mutually satisfying relationship between man and woman. His nearest approach to date is the portrayal of the primitives Lok and Fa in *The Inheritors;* but in the case of fully rational beings, we have only Sammy's assertions about the joy he shares with Taffy and Oliver's presumably happy marriage with a woman whom we never really see. Aside from these instances, lust replaces love as Golding's figures remain trapped within their selves.

Whatever the techniques and materials to which Golding may turn in the future, however, the difficulty of the novels which he has published since *Lord of the Flies*—even of *The Pyramid* in its own way—makes it unlikely that those now available will ever speak so immediately to the public as did his first book. Surely the religious orientation in many of his stories works to some degree against his popular success at present, with some readers put off by the orientation itself and others by his unwillingness to provide a comfortably doctrinal solution to the problems of his characters. Yet one may hope that Golding's candor in representing the extraordinary capacities and unavoidable limitations of man will win for his fiction a growing body of readers as time goes on. For his novels are relevant to us on the same grounds that the living novels of the past are relevant: as passionate and intelligent assessments of man's enduring condition. In short, the work published to date reveals Golding as more than a talented contemporary: as a man with important things to say, endowed with deeply original and compelling ways of saying them. And on the evidence of the radical shift in mode manifest in *The Pyramid*, he continues refusing to stand pat as a novelist, a fact which invites one to look forward with the keenest interest to the fictions he has yet to create.

1. Quoted in E. L. Epstein's "Notes" to *Lord of the Flies*, p. 250.

Index